G000168695

WALKING
THE LITERARY
LANDSCAPE

20 CLASSIC WALKS FOR BOOK-LOVERS
IN NORTHERN ENGLAND

VERTEBRATE PUBLISHING

Vertebrate Publishing, Sheffield
www.v-publishing.co.uk

WALKING
THE LITERARY
LANDSCAPE

20 CLASSIC WALKS FOR BOOK-LOVERS
IN NORTHERN ENGLAND

IAN HAMILTON | **DIANE ROBERTS**

WALKING
THE LITERARY
LANDSCAPE

20 CLASSIC WALKS FOR BOOK-LOVERS
IN NORTHERN ENGLAND

VG Copyright © 2014 Vertebrate Graphics Ltd and Ian Hamilton & Diane Roberts.

VP First published in 2014 by Vertebrate Publishing.

All rights reserved. No part of this work covered by the copyright hereon may be reproduced or used in any form or by any means – graphic, electronic, or mechanised, including photocopying, recording, taping, or information storage and retrieval systems – without the written permission of the publisher.

ISBN 978-1-906148-78-2

Cover photo: View of Top Withens near Haworth, West Yorkshire. Said to be the inspiration for the location Wuthering Heights in the novel of the same name by Emily Brontë.
Photo by: Diane Roberts.
All other photos by Diane Roberts, Dave Lee and Ann Hamilton.

All maps reproduced by permission of Ordnance Survey on behalf of The Controller of Her Majesty's Stationery Office. © Crown Copyright. 100025218

Design and production by Nathan Ryder – www.v-graphics.co.uk
Printed in China.

Every effort has been made to achieve accuracy of information in this guidebook. The authors, publishers and copyright owners can take no responsibility for: loss or injury (including fatal) to persons; loss or damage to property or equipment; trespass, irresponsible behaviour or any other mishap that may be suffered as a result of following the route descriptions or advice offered in this guidebook. The inclusion of a track or path as part of a route, or otherwise recommended, in this guidebook does not guarantee that the track or path will remain a Right of Way. If conflict with landowners arises we advise that you act politely and leave by the shortest route available. If the matter needs to be taken further then please take it up with the relevant authority.

Contents

Introduction vii
Acknowledgements viii
About the walks viii
Walk times viii
Navigation viii
Footpaths and rights of way ix

Safety ix
The Countryside Code ix
How to use this book xii
Maps, descriptions, distances xii
Km/mile conversion chart xiii
Area map xiv

THE LAKE DISTRICT

1 ..... Bassenthwaite Lake & Dodd *(Alfred, Lord Tennyson)* – **7.5km/4.6miles** 5
2 ..... Carrock Fell *(Charles Dickens)* – **5.2km/3.2miles** 9
3 ..... Coniston Water & Torver *(Arthur Ransome)* – **11km/7miles** 13
4 ..... Far Sawrey & Windermere *(Beatrix Potter)* – **13km/8miles** 19
5 ..... Grasmere & Rydal Water *(William Wordsworth)* – **9.7km/6miles** 25
6 ..... Walla Crag & Derwentwater *(John Ruskin)* – **8.4km/5.2miles** 29

THE NORTH EAST, THE MOORS & THE DALES

7 ..... Blanchland *(W. H. Auden)* – **5.6km/3.5miles** 39
8 ..... Humbleton Hill & Wooler *(William Shakespeare)* – **7km/4.3miles** 43
9 ..... Cleadon Hills & Marsden Rock *(Catherine Cookson)* – **10.5km/6.5miles** 47
10 ... Whitby *(Bram Stoker)* – **9.5km/6miles** 51
11 ... Around Thirsk *(James Herriot)* – **8km/5miles** 55
12 ... Upper Wharfedale & Hubberholme *(J. B. Priestley)* – **7km/4.5miles** 61
13 ... Malham Tarn & Cove *(Charles Kingsley)* – **14.7km/9.1miles** 65

PEAK DISTRICT, SOUTH PENNINES & CHESHIRE

14 ... Hurst Green & Stonyhurst College *(J. R. R. Tolkien)* – **10.5km/6.5miles** 75
15 ... Haworth & the moors *(The Brontë sisters)* – **14km/8.7miles** 81
16 ... Mytholmroyd & the Calder Valley *(Ted Hughes)* – **9.5km/6miles** 87
17 ... Mam Tor & the caverns *(Arthur Conan Doyle)* – **8km/5miles** 91
18 ... Around Chatsworth *(Jane Austen)* – **8km/5miles** 95
19 ... Knutsford & Tatton Park *(Elizabeth Gaskell)* – **11km/7miles** 99
20 ... Daresbury *(Lewis Carroll)* – **8km/5miles** 105

Appendix 108
About the authors 112

MALHAM COVE (ROUTE 13)

INTRODUCTION

Literature and a love of the landscape walk hand in hand. Great writers show us the physical world through new eyes and inspire affection for what might be familiar sights.

Some scenes are burned into our collective memory – daffodils dancing in the Lakeland breeze or the wind whipping the moors above Haworth.

Our book takes you to the source of inspiration for these and other literary landmarks in northern England. There are 20 walks in total, all of which can be managed by the reasonably fit walker and some are particularly suitable for children.

In fact, the idea for the book came during an outing near Stonyhurst College in Lancashire. Enthusiasm for the six-mile walk was waning among younger members of the party when one of the grown-ups mentioned that the man who wrote *The Lord of the Rings* had lived and taught nearby.

This was at the height at the popularity of Peter Jackson's trilogy of films and our Sunday afternoon stroll turned into a journey of adventure through Middle Earth.

When the two of us put our heads together we realised that while some of the books on our shelves made literary references, none brought together walking and literature in a single book.

Some of the walks leapt out at us, others took a bit of hunting down. Like many people we'd associated Sir Arthur Conan Doyle with the Sherlock Holmes stories but, though familiar with the show caves around Castleton, we didn't know that his short story *The Terror of Blue John Gap* was written after Conan Doyle made a convalescent stay in the Peak District.

Or that Charles Dickens, a tireless walker around the streets of London and his beloved Kent, had made an ill-fated venture on one of the Lake District's lesser known fells with his friend and fellow writer Wilkie Collins.

We hope you enjoy the stories behind the walks. Most of all, we hope you and your walking companions – young and old, human and canine – find inspiration in the countryside that inspired some of our greatest literature.

Diane Roberts and Ian Hamilton

ACKNOWLEDGEMENTS

The authors would like to thank the following for their help:

Dave Lee for support, patience and creative direction; Ann Hamilton for constant encouragement and countless cups of tea; Ed Hamilton for breaking his weekend sleep pattern to provide cheerfulness throughout; Jill for her eye for detail; Anne, Joe, Winn, the Lees and James-Lees for their encouragement and for looking after Reggie!

Fellow walkers Emma Buchanan, Davinia and Charlie, Joe, Pat and Tanya, Liz, Jon, Sue and Miles, and walking club members Gill, PT, Mary and Kris; David and the team for their enthusiasm and support.

ABOUT THE WALKS

All the walks in this book can be completed in less than four hours and most are suitable for family groups. The majority use clearly defined paths and where climbing is involved it is not generally beyond the capability of a reasonably fit walker.

However, some are across rough country and the length of a particular walk is no guarantee of its suitability for all. Indeed, the shortest – Carrock Fell – is in many ways the most testing and shouldn't be taken on by anyone in poor visibility.

The route description for each walk should be studied carefully before setting out.

WALK TIMES

The times given for each walk take account of a short stop for a sandwich and hot drink but not (where applicable) for a pub lunch. You will need to adjust accordingly if you plan a break of longer than 20 minutes

NAVIGATION

The route description and accompanying map should be sufficient to complete most if not all of the walks in this book. It is always a good idea, however, to carry the relevant map in the Ordnance Survey Explorer series in case you need to cut short the walk or take an alternative route. The maps are listed with each walk.

For fell top and moorland walks a reasonable level of map reading ability and competence in use of a compass is strongly advised. A GPS (Global Positioning System) is good for locating position but does not compensate for poor navigational skills.

MOBILE PHONES

Remember that mobile phone reception may be limited on some of the walks.

FOOTPATHS AND RIGHTS OF WAY

All the walks in the book follow public rights of way or other routes with public access, including 'permitted' or 'concession' footpaths.

SAFETY

It is strongly advised that appropriate footwear is used – walking boots designed to provide stability and security on uneven and slippery terrain. A waterproof, windproof jacket is essential and waterproof overtrousers or trousers are strongly recommended.

Sufficient insulating clothing should also be worn or carried that is appropriate to the type of walk planned and the time of year. Carry lots of food and drink, including an emergency supply. It's surprising how quickly you can become depleted and/or dehydrated, especially at the end of the day.

MOUNTAIN RESCUE

In case of accident or similar need requiring mountain rescue assistance, dial 999 and ask for **POLICE – MOUNTAIN RESCUE**. Be prepared to give a 6-figure grid reference of your position.

THE COUNTRYSIDE CODE

Be safe – plan ahead.

Even when going out locally, it's best to get the latest information about where and when you can go; for example, your rights to go onto some areas of open land may be restricted while work is carried out, for safety reasons or during breeding and shooting seasons. Follow advice and local signs, and be prepared for the unexpected.

» Refer to up-to-date maps or guidebooks.

» You're responsible for your own safety and for others in your care, so be prepared for changes in weather and other events.

» There are many organisations offering specific advice on equipment and safety; contact visitor information centres and libraries for a list of outdoor recreation groups.

» Check weather forecasts before you leave, and don't be afraid to turn back.

» Part of the appeal of the countryside is that you can get away from it all. You may not see anyone for hours and there are many places without clear mobile phone signals, so let someone else know where you're going and when you expect to return.

LEAVE GATES AND PROPERTY AS YOU FIND THEM
Please respect the working life of the countryside as our actions can affect people's livelihoods, our heritage, and the safety and welfare of animals and ourselves.

» A farmer will normally leave a gate closed to keep livestock in, but may sometimes leave it open so they can reach food and water. Leave gates as you find them or follow instructions on signs; if walking in a group, make sure the last person knows how to leave the gates.

» In fields where crops are growing, follow the paths wherever possible.

» Use gates and stiles – climbing over walls, hedges and fences can damage them and increase the risk of farm animals escaping.

» Our heritage belongs to all of us – be careful not to disturb ruins and historic sites.

» Leave machinery and livestock alone – don't interfere with animals even if you think they're in distress. Try to alert the farmer instead.

PROTECT PLANTS AND ANIMALS, AND TAKE YOUR LITTER HOME
We have a responsibility to protect our countryside now and for future generations, so make sure you don't harm animals, birds, plants or trees.

» Litter and leftover food doesn't just spoil the beauty of the countryside, it can be dangerous to wildlife and farm animals and can spread disease. Take your litter home with you. Dropping litter and dumping rubbish are criminal offences.

» Discover the beauty of the natural environment and take special care not to damage, destroy or remove features such as rocks, plants and trees. They provide homes and food for wildlife, and add to everybody's enjoyment of the countryside.

» Wild animals and farm animals can behave unpredictably if you get too close, especially if they're with their young – so give them plenty of space.

» Fires can be as devastating to wildlife and habitats as they are to people and property – so be careful not to drop a match or smouldering cigarette at any time of the year. Sometimes, controlled fires are used to manage vegetation, particularly on heaths and moors between October and early April, so please check that a fire is not supervised before calling 999.

KEEP DOGS UNDER CLOSE CONTROL

The countryside is a great place to exercise dogs, but it is the owner's duty to make sure their dog is not a danger or nuisance to farm animals, wildlife or other people.

» By law, you must control your dog so that it does not disturb or scare farm animals or wildlife. You must keep your dog on a short lead on most areas of open country and common land between 1 March and 31 July, and at all times near farm animals.

» You do not have to put your dog on a lead on public paths as long as it is under close control. But as a general rule, keep your dog on a lead if you cannot rely on its obedience. By law, farmers are entitled to destroy a dog that injures or worries their animals.

» If a farm animal chases you and your dog, it is safer to let your dog off the lead – don't risk getting hurt by trying to protect it.

» Take particular care that your dog doesn't scare sheep and lambs or wander where it might disturb birds that nest on the ground and other wildlife – eggs and young will soon die without protection from their parents.

» Everyone knows how unpleasant dog mess is and it can cause infections – so always clean up after your dog and get rid of the mess responsibly. Also make sure your dog is wormed regularly.

CONSIDER OTHER PEOPLE

Showing consideration and respect for other people makes the countryside a pleasant environment for everyone – at home, at work and at leisure.

» Busy traffic on small country roads can be unpleasant and dangerous to local people, visitors and wildlife – so slow down and, where possible, leave your vehicle at home, consider sharing lifts and use alternatives such as public transport or cycling. For public transport information, phone Traveline on 0871 200 2233.

» Respect the needs of local people – for example, don't block gateways, driveways or other entry points with your vehicle.

» Keep out of the way when farm animals are being gathered or moved and follow directions from the farmer.

» Support the rural economy – for example, buy your supplies from local shops.

HOW TO USE THIS BOOK

This book should provide you with all of the information that you need for an enjoyable, trouble free and successful walk. The following tips should also be of help:

1. We strongly recommend that you invest in the maps listed with each route. These are essential even if you are familiar with the area – you may need to cut short the walk or take an alternative route.

2. Choose your route. Consider the time you have available and the abilities/level of experience of all members of your party – the read the safety section of this book.

3. We recommend that you study the route description carefully before setting off. Cross-reference this to your OS map so that you've got a good sense of general orientation in case you need an escape route. Make sure that you are familiar with the symbols used on the maps.

4. Get out there and get walking!

MAPS, DESCRIPTIONS, DISTANCES

While every effort has been made to maintain accuracy within the maps and descriptions in this guide, we have had to process a vast amount of information and we are unable to guarantee that every single detail is correct.

Please exercise caution if a direction appears at odds with the route on the map. If in doubt, a comparison between the route, the description and a quick cross-reference to your OS map (along with a bit of common sense) should help ensure that you're on the right track. Note that distances have been measured off the map, and map distances rarely coincide 100% with distances on the ground. Please treat stated distances as a guideline only.

Ordnance Survey maps are the most commonly used, are easy to read and many people are happy using them. If you're not familiar with OS maps and are unsure of what the symbols mean, you can download a free OS 1:25,000 map legend from **www.v-publishing.co.uk**

KM/MILE CONVERSION CHART

METRIC TO IMPERIAL
1 kilometre [km]	1000 m	0.6214 mile
1 metre [m]	100 cm	1.0936 yd
1 centimetre [cm]	10 mm	0.3937 in
1 millimetre [mm]		0.03937 in

IMPERIAL TO METRIC
1 mile	1760 yd	1.6093 km
1 yard [yd]	3 ft	0.9144 m
1 foot [ft]	12 in	0.3048 m
1 inch [in]		2.54 cm

To help you, here are a few of the symbols and abbreviations that we use on the maps and in the directions:

 ROUTE STARTING POINT   ROUTE MARKER    OPTIONAL ROUTE

 ROUTE DIRECTION   GR = grid reference.

WALKING THE LITERARY LANDSCAPE

THE LAKE DISTRICT

1	Bassenthwaite Lake & Dodd	5
2	Carrock Fell	9
3	Coniston Water & Torver	13
4	Far Sawrey & Windermere	19
5	Grasmere & Rydal Water	25
6	Walla Crag & Derwentwater	29

THE NORTH EAST, THE MOORS & THE DALES

7	Blanchland	39
8	Humbleton Hill & Wooler	43
9	Cleadon Hills & Marsden Rock	47
10	Whitby	51
11	Around Thirsk	55
12	Upper Wharfedale & Hubberholme	61
13	Malham Tarn & Cove	65

PEAK DISTRICT, SOUTH PENNINES & CHESHIRE

14	Hurst Green & Stonyhurst College	75
15	Haworth & the moors	81
16	Mytholmroyd & the Calder Valley	87
17	Mam Tor & the caverns	91
18	Around Chatsworth	95
19	Knutsford & Tatton Park	99
20	Daresbury	105

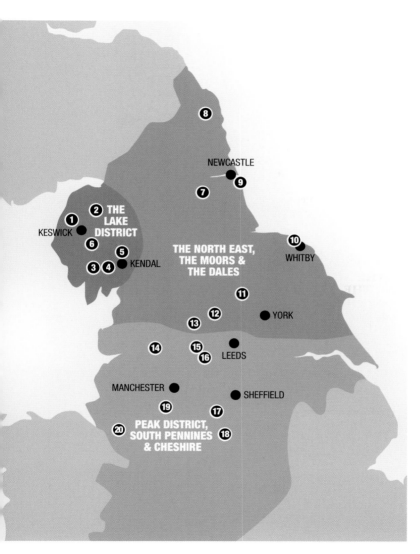

AREA MAP

The Lake District

England's only 'mountainous' region. Home to the highest peaks and deepest lakes, to golden eagles and ospreys and to woodland, open fells and rocky tops, it's no wonder that countless writers have found inspiration here.

DOVE COTTAGE (ROUTE 5)

MIREHOUSE

1 Bassenthwaite Lake & Dodd
(Alfred, Lord Tennyson)

7.5km/4.6miles

A bird's eye view of the lake with poetic links to the Arthurian legend and back down to earth with a visit to a delightful country church.

Dodd Wood • Dodd summit • Dodd Wood • Mirehouse • St Bega's Church • Dodd Wood

START
The walk starts in the Forestry Commission car park at Dodd Wood on the A591 north of Keswick. GR: NY 235 282.

THE WALK
Few images in English poetry are as evocative as that of the woman's arm 'clothed in white samite, mystic, wonderful' which emerged from the lake to hand King Arthur his sword Excalibur – and to reclaim it at the end of his life.

Alfred, Lord Tennyson's poem *Morte d'Arthur*, once a favourite of English teachers everywhere, has particular resonance for lovers of Bassenthwaite Lake in Cumbria where Tennyson stayed and from which he drew inspiration for his epic work.

Tennyson was a guest of the Spedding family at Mirehouse, which still stands close to the lake shore. Today, almost 180 years on, his connection to the country house is celebrated in an annual poetry competition and a 'poetry walk' through the grounds.

But anyone gazing over the still waters of Bassenthwaite on a summer's afternoon will sense the air of mystery and romance that Tennyson must have felt when he looked out on the same view in Victorian times.

This is a walk of two halves. The first is a straightforward (if reasonably strenuous) climb through trees to the summit of Dodd and a panoramic view of the lake and surrounding fells; the second, a gentle stroll past Mirehouse to St Bega's Church, believed to be the 'chapel nigh the field' the poet described in the opening lines of *Morte d'Arthur*.

Both walks start and finish at the Forestry Commission car park at Dodd Wood and can be taken in either order. During summer months the house and gardens at Mirehouse are also opened to the public by the Spedding family whose ancestor James was a friend of Tennyson's and who accompanied him on his walks along the shores of Bassenthwaite. There is an entrance fee.

Route finding is generally easy and in places made easier by coloured waymarkers.

DISTANCE: 7.5KM/4.6MILES   **TOTAL ASCENT**: 402M/1318FT   **START**: DODD WOOD CAR PARK (GR: NY 235 282)
TIME: 2½ HOURS   **MAP**: OS EXPLORER OL4: THE ENGLISH LAKES (NORTH WESTERN AREA) 1:25,000
REFRESHMENTS: SAWMILL TEAROOM AT START   **NAVIGATION**: CLEAR PATHS AND TRACKS
SUGGESTED READING: *SELECTED POEMS*, TENNYSON (PUBLISHED BY PENGUIN CLASSICS)

Directions – Bassenthwaite Lake & Dodd

S→ Cross the footbridge behind the tearoom and climb on a clear path until, after a short distance, you reach a forest lane. Turn **right** and follow as the lane climbs steeply through trees. As you gain height Skill Beck can be heard below to your right.

2 After half a mile the lane emerges from the trees and continues to climb through a cleared area, eventually joining a track from the left. Shortly after passing a second junction take a **right fork**, signposted *Dodd Summit*, off the main track.

3 Pass the bench (which affords a fine view towards Derwentwater) the track swings right before climbing again. **Ignore** the green waymarker sign to your left and instead follow the main track to the summit.

Looking down from the summit in a north-westerly direction you will see Mirehouse and, between that and the lake, the tiny church of St Bega's.

4 **Retrace** your steps as far as the green waymarker, this time following it **right** towards a second bench again with excellent views. Just before the bench the track drops down right, eventually re-entering trees with Bassenthwaite Lake to your left.

5 At a wide track turn **right** and then **left** at the next junction (still following the green waymarker). At the next junction turn **right** and follow the track as it drops down towards the road and car park with Skill Beck now on your right.

6 Cross the main road **with care** and go through a gate to the left of the visitor entrance to Mirehouse. Follow the public footpath as it skirts the main house until a track **forks left** opposite the entrance to the grounds.

7 Follow the path down to a second gate and continue **straight ahead** across a field towards St Bega's Church and Bassenthwaite Lake.

8 After visiting the church **retrace** your steps to the car park, pausing to enjoy the sight of Mirehouse nestled beneath the protective bulk of Dodd.

MIREHOUSE

Mirehouse has connections with many of the great names of art and literature from the last 200 years. Tennyson, Wordsworth, Robert Southey, Edward Fitzgerald, Thomas Carlyle and John Constable were all friends of the Spedding family and there are letters and manuscripts by them on display at the house. A small open-air theatre was opened at Mirehouse in 1974 for a reading of *Morte d'Arthur* to the Tennyson Society.

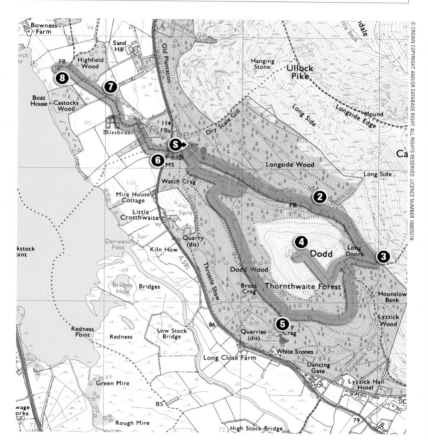

© CROWN COPYRIGHT AND/OR DATABASE RIGHT. ALL RIGHTS RESERVED. LICENCE NUMBER 100025218.

1 BASSENTHWAITE LAKE & DODD

2 Carrock Fell
(Charles Dickens)

5.2km/3.2miles

An ascent of one of Lakeland's outlying fells, famed for its geology and connection with Charles Dickens.

Mosedale • Carrock Fell • Stone Ends • Mosedale

START

The walk starts at the red telephone box in Mosedale, best reached off the A66 between Penrith and Keswick (GR: NY 357 323). There is parking on the roadside on the approaches to the village.

THE WALK

When Charles Dickens wasn't writing some of the greatest novels in the English language, or finding shelter for the fallen women of Victorian England, or performing in the theatre, or eating, drinking and enjoying good company, or providing guidance for his wife and 10 children, he was as often as not out walking.

But his visit to Cumberland in 1857 with literary soulmate Wilkie Collins (author of the first English detective novel) gives us a rare recorded example of Dickens enjoying the pleasures of walking in northern England.

Their choice of Lakeland outing was a curious one and does make you wonder whether the locals were having a joke at the visitors' expense. Carrock Fell is not one of those ever likely to be overrun by tourists, especially those visiting the Lakes on holiday for the first time. It is attractive mainly to the keen geologist who will no doubt be fascinated by the very rocks and stones the rest of us find a hazard.

But what Dickens and Collins describe as a 'trumpery little mountain' offers not just a physical (and navigational) challenge but rewards those who reach its summit with a delightful cairn and splendid views over some of its better known neighbours.

Our route favours the less popular ascent from Mosedale, a climb steep enough in its initial stages without the distractions of bracken, gorse and scree. But with the rapid gain in height comes a fine view, along the path of the River Caldew and, eventually, to Sharp Edge and Blencathra beyond.

Having reached the first of these false tops you'll find the going much easier. Route finding remains a challenge if you are to avoid clambering over knee-high clumps of heather (word of warning – Wilkie Collins needed medical treatment after spraining his ankle on the walk).

NB Sections of the walk are steep and rocky. Route finding needs care throughout. Not to be undertaken in mist.

DISTANCE: 5.2KM/3.2MILES   **TOTAL ASCENT**: 425M/1394FT   **START**: MOSEDALE VILLAGE (GR: NY 357 323)
TIME: 3 HOURS   **MAP**: OS EXPLORER OL5: THE ENGLISH LAKES (NORTH EASTERN AREA) 1:25,000
REFRESHMENTS: MILL INN, MUNGRISDALE   **NAVIGATION**: ROUTE FINDING NEEDS CARE ON ASCENT
AND AT HIGHER LEVEL. NOT TO BE UNDERTAKEN IN MIST   **SUGGESTED READING**: *LAZY TOUR OF
TWO IDLE APPRENTICES*, CHARLES DICKENS AND WILKIE COLLINS (AVAILABLE FREE TO DOWNLOAD)

Directions – Carrock Fell

S→ From the red telephone box in Mosedale turn **left** along a metalled road marked Swine-side. After 100 metres turn **right** at the corner of a stone wall (just before a sign for Mosedale House) and head up the fell on a footpath through the bracken.

2 **Stay right** as the footpath presents two options right and left in quick succession and continue to climb through bracken and gorse. The path becomes indistinct in places, particularly as it crosses patches of scree, but maintain your upward (and fairly steep) climb until a beech tree and sapling come into view.

3 **Keep left** above the tree and follow a clearer path until you reach a stone shelter (bield in Wainwright's description). Beyond the shelter the path levels and after a short while passes a cairn above on the left. A detour to the cairn affords a splendid view towards Bowscale Fell and Blencathra.

4 **Return** to your path from the cairn **keeping left** when it meets your upward route and taking especial care in the initial stages to stay on course. The path becomes more defined as it passes to the left of a first rocky outcrop and swings to the right of a second.

5 As the climb becomes steeper (and the going underfoot boggier) the ruins of an ancient hill fort that guards the summit of the fell come clearly into view. Eventually the path is joined by a stream.

6 Close up the ruins bring an air of mystery to the summit. Without doubt they offer a superb vantage point for any lookout scanning the surrounding country for an invading army. From here the Scottish border looks within touching distance.

7 Follow a clear path **east** from the summit to a cairn on the edge of the plateau. This descends steeply through rocks swinging left past a broken sheepfold to reach the top of Further Gill gully.

8 **Climb with care** into the gully and follow clear steps to a defined footpath with a stream tumbling down to your right. The path turns left beneath scree to pick up Rake Trod.

CARROCK FELL

Dickens was an enthusiastic – not to say compulsive – walker who often took to the streets at night to relieve the troubles of the day. His nocturnal rambles could cover distances of up to 30 miles and, as his essay *Night Walks* reveals, gave him a remarkable insight into the plight of London's homeless. Wilkie Collins, Dickens's companion on Carrock Fell, was a more grudging exponent of the benefits of walking, once writing 'The worst curse of human life is the detestable necessity of taking exercise.'

9 The road and path ahead are now clearly in view. Towards the road the grassy path passes a quarry, the remains of Carrock End Mine.

10 Turn **right** at the road passing Stone Ends on the way to Mosedale and your car.

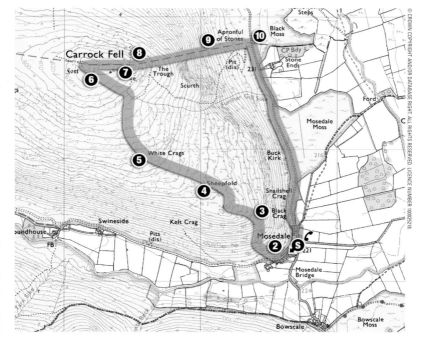

© CROWN COPYRIGHT AND/OR DATABASE RIGHT. ALL RIGHTS RESERVED. LICENCE NUMBER 100025218.

2 CARROCK FELL

3 Coniston Water & Torver
(Arthur Ransome)

11km/7miles

A stroll through the Lakeland scenery that inspired *Swallows and Amazons*.

Torver • Coniston Water • Torver Commons • Torver

START

Park in the Lake District National Park car park (opposite the Land Rover garage) on the A5084 just outside Torver. GR: SD 287 933.

THE WALK

Arthur Ransome's adventure stories are the perfect blend of childhood innocence and good old-fashioned derring-do. But for sheer intrigue his own career as a foreign correspondent takes a bit of beating.

Ransome had a front seat at the Russian Revolution and, through his second wife Evgenia, became close to Lenin and Trotsky. So close, in fact, that he never really escaped suspicion of being a spy.

Writing and journalism was not his first choice of occupation. He studied chemistry at university – not very successfully – and landed a job as an office junior at a publishing house in London.

Here, surrounded by creative talent, he began his first book, a study of London's artistic and literary set, published in 1907 under the title of *Bohemia in London*. He went on to write biographies of literary figures like Oscar Wilde, Robert Louis Stevenson and Edgar Allan Poe.

Throughout his career, he harboured an affection for the Lake District, where he had been educated and where – at Nibthwaite on Coniston Water – he spent summer holidays as a child.

When he returned to England after his spell in Russia he worked part-time for the *Manchester Guardian* and moved to the Lakes. Inspired by the scenery he knew as a child he produced his best known work – the series of children's books, *Swallows and Amazons*.

These books follow the adventures of the Walker children – the Swallows – on holiday in the Lakes and recount their rivalry on water and dry land with the Blacketts – the Amazons – and, not least, local pirate Captain Flint.

The walk takes in Coniston Water, views of the Old Man of Coniston, Torver Village and Torver Commons.

DISTANCE: 11KM/7MILES **TOTAL ASCENT**: 130M/426FT **START**: LAKE DISTRICT NATIONAL PARK CAR PARK (GR: SD 287 933) **TIME**: 3½ HOURS **MAP**: OS EXPLORER OL6: THE LAKE DISTRICT (SOUTH WESTERN AREA) 1:25,000 **REFRESHMENTS**: TEAROOMS AND PUBS IN TORVER VILLAGE **NAVIGATION**: CLEAR PATHS PASSING THROUGH SOME FARMLAND THAT CAN BE MUDDY IN PLACES **SUGGESTED READING**: *SWALLOWS AND AMAZONS*, ARTHUR RANSOME (PUBLISHED BY VINTAGE CHILDREN'S CLASSICS)

Directions – Coniston Water & Torver

S⟶ From the car park, turn **left** and follow the road as it descends until you reach a sign for Torver Commons. Here follow the footpath (signposted *Coniston via The Lake Shore*), pass through a kissing gate and continue along the path to get your first glimpse of Coniston Water to the right.

2 **Continue** along the path passing Coniston launch. Along the lake shore the path is well defined but you may encounter rivulets running into the lake and juniper bushes. Keep to the path as it winds around the lake until you pass through two gates signposted *Lake District National Park*, the second in a stone wall next to the lake.

3 Shortly after passing through the gate you will come to a junction. Take the footpath to the **right** marked *Cumbria Way*. Pass through another gate in a wall and walk through a clearing to the left. At a waymark sign take the path to the **left**, walking up through woodland towards a stone wall and away from the lake.

4 **Follow the path** as it ascends and passes through a gap in the wall, **ignoring any turnings** until you reach a gate. Continue ahead through woodland (with a stream running to your right) and follow the track as it ascends quite steeply and veers to the left. Keep the wall to your right, **ignoring** a higher path, and continue along the main path until you reach two gates, after the second of which you will see the Old Man of Coniston.

5 Keep to the path, passing through a gate and then a kissing gate. You will pass farmland as the path turns left. At the end of the path, **cross** the track and follow a public footpath sign across a stile into a field and through a series of small stone stiles. In the final field you will see a metal kissing gate in the far right corner.

PEEL ISLAND

Peel Island, which lies at the southern end of Coniston Water, is widely thought to have been the model for Wild Cat Island in Arthur Ransome's most famous adventure story – *Swallows and Amazons*. Ransome wrote affectionately about the island in his autobiography, describing it as a 'crystallising point for happy memories', and even took a stone from the island to Russia to remind himself of his spiritual home. Today Peel Island is owned by the National Trust.

6 Turn **left** after the kissing gate, crossing over the stone bridge and follow the road as it curves right into Torver Village, passing the Parish Church and the Wilson Arms pub on the right. Just past the pub follow the lane **ahead** to pass some houses. Follow the footpath through a **gate to the left** and cross a field before meeting the main road.

7 Cross the road and a stile opposite and follow the path over a footbridge. Cross a second stile and walk across a field to the far right to pass through a gate on to a narrow lane. Pass through a wooden gate signposted *Public Bridleway Mill Brow*.

8 Follow the path with a stream running to the left, and pass through three gates. After the third gate (**ignoring** the bridge to the left) take the **path ahead to the right**. Pass through a gate onto Torver Commons and follow the public footpath to the right. When you reach a series of overhead cables take a left turn and follow the path running in parallel with the cables.

9 A disused reservoir will come into view on the right. Continue to follow the path until you reach a dam at the end of the reservoir. Here turn **left** along a path, lined by trees with Torver Beck to the right, eventually crossing the beck and passing through a kissing gate to reach the main road.

10 Turn **left** and follow the road round until you reach the car park on the right.

TORVER BECK

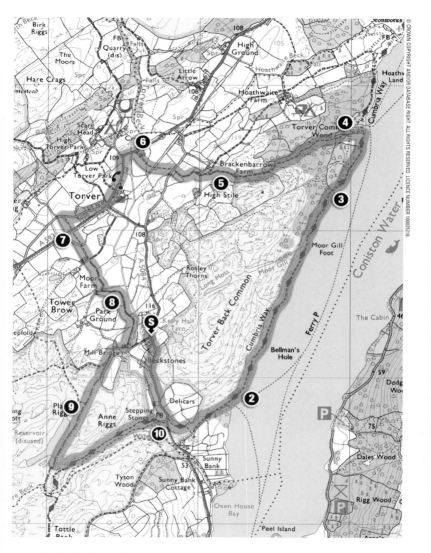

3 CONISTON WATER & TORVER

© CROWN COPYRIGHT AND/OR DATABASE RIGHT ALL RIGHTS RESERVED LICENCE NUMBER 100025218.

WINDERMERE FROM CLAIFE HEIGHTS

4 Far Sawrey & Windermere
(Beatrix Potter)

13km/8miles

A walk through the Lakeland landscape Beatrix Potter bequeathed to the nation.

Far Sawrey • Claife Heights • Windermere • Near Sawrey • Hill Top • Far Sawrey

START

Park in the village hall car park at Far Sawrey on B5285 road to Hawkshead just past Cuckoo Brow Inn. GR: SD 379 954.

THE WALK

The story of Beatrix Potter is woven into the fabric of the Lake District. But were it not for a young publisher called Norman Warne we might never have heard of Peter Rabbit, and Cumbria would have lost one of its greatest benefactors.

Beatrix first came to the Lake District on a family holiday from London. Sheltered and isolated, enjoying the company mainly of her brother Bertram and a multitude of family pets, she found freedom in the countryside and artistic release in sketching and drawing.

The rabbits and mice that had been her constant companions in Kensington soon began to feature in her work and Peter Rabbit, her most famous creation, first appeared in an illustrated letter to a friend's five year old son.

Having been rejected by publishers Frederick Warne and Co and having decided to publish the story of Peter Rabbit herself, Beatrix found an unexpected ally in the youngest of the three Warne brothers – Norman – who insisted that the company reverse its earlier decision.

For a while it seemed the real-life story of the rather lonely spinster would have a happy ending. The couple fell in love, became engaged and prepared for publication of a book that would both make her fortune and forge a remarkable international reputation.

Tragically, Norman died before they could be married and Beatrix retreated to her beloved Lake District to produce a series of books which have delighted children ever since. The small farm she bought – Hill Top – provides the setting for stories featuring many of her best-loved characters, including Tom Kitten, Jemima Puddle-duck and Samuel Whiskers.

She became immersed in country life and conservation and on her death left a substantial amount of property and land to the National Trust, a legacy every bit as important as that of her books.

The walk starts at Far Sawrey, ascends Claife Heights, and continues along the shore of Lake Windermere before returning to Near Sawrey and Hill Top.

DISTANCE: 13 KM/8MILES **TOTAL ASCENT**: 140M/459FT **START**: FAR SAWREY VILLAGE HALL CAR PARK
(GR: SD 379 954) **TIME**: 3 HOURS **MAP**: OS EXPLORER OL7: THE LAKE DISTRICT (SOUTH EASTERN AREA) 1:25,000
REFRESHMENTS: PUBS AND TEAROOMS IN NEAR AND FAR SAWREY **NAVIGATION**: CLEAR PATHS, STRENUOUS
IN PARTS AND SOME ROAD WALKING IN BUSY TOURIST AREA **SUGGESTED READING**: *THE TALE OF PETER RABBIT,*
BEATRIX POTTER (PUBLISHED BY WARNE)

Directions – Far Sawrey & Windermere

S➜ **Cross** the road from the car park and take the footpath **ahead** (signposted *Public Bridleway Belle Grange 3 miles*) passing Sawrey Institute on the right. Pass through a wooden gate and follow the path as it curves to the right. After the gate there is a way sign and, where the path forks, continue to follow the path **to the right** until you reach a wooden gate and a signpost. Continue **straight ahead**, signposted *Public Bridleway, Windermere, Lakeshore Ferry* (ignoring the path to the left).

❷ Continue **straight ahead** passing through another wooden gate and following the path with a wood to your right. At a signpost to the ferry (marked with a yellow arrow) pass through a gate and enter a wood keeping to a narrow winding path and crossing a small brook.

❸ Continue along the narrow path as it descends down two sets of wooden steps past Claife Station and then by stone steps to the main road. **Cross the road with care** and take the off road path through a gate signposted *Near Sawrey and Hill Top.*

❹ On leaving the footpath take an **immediate left**, passing a house named 'The Ridings'. At the top of the road turn **left** and continue to descend, passing a sign for *Cunsey*. The road slopes to the right and after passing a house called 'The Bield' on the left follow a sign marked *public footpath* to cross a small stone stile. Follow the path along the left of the field and continue to meet the lake shore.

❺ Continue along the path and over a wooden bridge with a gate. The path then passes through a kissing gate and across a small stone step stile. You will then cross a number of small wooden bridges and a wooden gate, passing a sign for *Rawlinson Nab*.

❻ Continue **straight on** and as the path broadens take the lower path as it turns to the right. Follow the path along the shoreline, crossing a wooden bridge. The path climbs to meet the main road at a stone step stile and then a wooden stile. Turn **right** and walk carefully along the road**.**

POTTER'S PROPERTIES

Beatrix Potter is most readily associated with Hill Top, but the writer owned a number of small farms and other properties in and around Sawrey. In fact she lived most of the time before her marriage at Castle Farm, which she bought in 1909, and from where she would walk the short distance to Hill Top to write her children's books. When at the age of 47 she married William Heelis and moved to the Lake District full-time, the couple lived at Castle Cottage, a bigger and more convenient house and another part of her growing portfolio of properties.

7 Immediately after passing Cunsey Lodge on the left follow the signpost marked *Public Bridleway*. Go **straight ahead** along the bridleway, **ignoring** the turning to the left through woodland. Keep to the path until you reach Cunsey Beck and here turn **left** to follow the path, keeping the beck to your right.

8 Pass through a wooden gate to leave the bridleway, turn **right** and walk along the road. After passing Eel House take an **immediate right** to follow a minor road, crossing the river at a small stone bridge and carry **straight on**, passing some stone cottages on the left. At the end of the road turn **right**, signposted *Near Sawrey*. You will pass the Sawrey House Hotel and, turning **right** at the end of the road, enter Near Sawrey, passing Hill Top, Beatrix Potter's farmhouse.

9 Shortly after Hill Top, pass through a National Trust gate (signposted *footpath to Far Sawrey*). Follow the path and pass through a gate and kissing gate, taking the path to the **left** that runs alongside the stream. Cross the bridge and follow the footpath through a field.

10 Leave the field through a kissing gate and turn **left**, walking carefully along the road to the top and turn **right**, walking past the Cuckoo Brow Inn on the left before returning to the car park.

HILL TOP

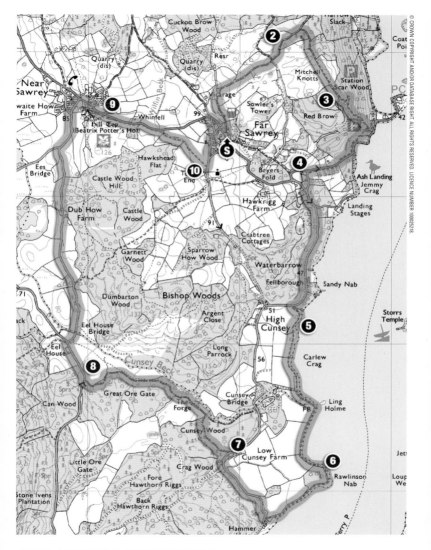

© CROWN COPYRIGHT AND/OR DATABASE RIGHT. ALL RIGHTS RESERVED. LICENCE NUMBER 100025218.

4 FAR SAWREY & WINDERMERE

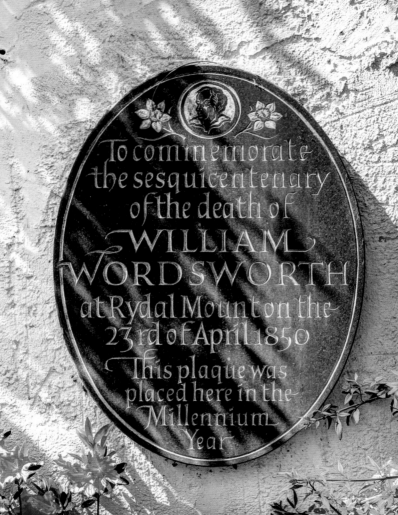

To commemorate
the sesquicentenary
of the death of
WILLIAM
WORDSWORTH
at Rydal Mount on the
23rd of April 1850
This plaque was
placed here in the
Millennium
Year

WORDSWORTH MEMORIAL PLAQUE AT RYDAL MOUNT

5 Grasmere & Rydal Water
(William Wordsworth)

9.7km/6miles

A walk that connects two of the poet's houses and takes in one of his favourite Lakeland views.

Grasmere • Dove Cottage • Rydal Mount • Pelter Bridge • Loughrigg Terrace • Grasmere

START

The walk starts in the village of Grasmere, a popular spot for lovers of Wordsworth, the Lakes and a certain brand of gingerbread. There is a large car park in the village. GR: NY 339 073.

THE WALK

If ever one man represented the close connection between walking and writing, it was William Wordsworth.

The poet drew the attention of the literary world to the natural beauty of this corner of northern England; he may never have heard of a place called Cumbria but more than 160 years after his death he remains its finest ambassador.

His fellow Lakeland resident Thomas de Quincey once felt obliged to point out that Wordsworth's legs had few admirers among members of the female sex.

But, whatever people thought of their shape, Wordsworth's legs carried him to remarkable heights of poetic inspiration – and over pretty much every blade of grass in the Lakes.

De Quincey estimated that in the course of his lifetime Wordsworth must have tramped more than 175,000 miles – a fair proportion of which would have been walks from the houses in Grasmere and Rydal where he lived for many years.

Our walk takes in those two houses – Dove Cottage and Rydal Mount – and the fine view over Grasmere from Loughrigg Terrace, a favourite haunt of the poet and his sister Dorothy.

Today the walk presents an additional challenge to that faced by the Wordsworths – the busy A591 which divides both houses from Rydal Water and Grasmere and which requires great care when crossing.

Otherwise, there is pretty much something for all ages here – fells reflected in the mirror-like calm of the waters below, a shoreline stroll, two caves to jolt the imagination of younger walkers, a picturesque packhorse bridge ... the list goes on.

And, of course, those two houses – both open to the public – where enthusiasts can get a flavour of what Wordsworth's life was like when he wasn't out and about putting those unshapely but extremely serviceable legs to good use.

There is no climbing to speak of and route finding is straightforward throughout.

DISTANCE: 9.7KM/6MILES   **TOTAL ASCENT**: 170M/557FT   **START**: GRASMERE PUBLIC CAR PARK (GR: NY 339 073).
TIME: 2½ HOURS   **MAP**: OS EXPLORER OL7: THE ENGLISH LAKES (SOUTH EASTERN AREA) 1:25,000
REFRESHMENTS: PUBS AND TEAROOMS IN GRASMERE AND RYDAL   **NAVIGATION**: STRAIGHTFORWARD
SUGGESTED READING: *SELECTED POEMS*, WILLIAM WORDSWORTH (PUBLISHED BY PENGUIN CLASSICS)

Directions – Grasmere & Rydal Water

➊➤ Turn **left** out of the car park crossing the A591 near a roundabout. Turn **right**, bearing **left** off the main road at the sign to Dove Cottage.

➋ Pass Dove Cottage on your left climbing a metalled road to a junction, following signposts marked *Coffin Route to Rydal*. This denotes the path taken by coffin-bearers from Rydal (where there was no burial ground) to Grasmere (where there was).

➌ The path swings right and continues through several gates, slowly gaining height above the busy road and gradually affording views towards Loughrigg Fell over the water on the other side. A terrace offers a couple of seats for just such a purpose.

➍ Towards Rydal the path becomes more even and passes above Rydal Mount on your right. Turn **right** in front of the house down a metalled road. You will pass the village church just before rejoining the A591.

➎ **Cross the road with care** and turn **left** following the pavement opposite for about 200 metres. Cross Pelter Bridge on your **right** and turn **immediate right** in front of Cote How car park, climbing gradually past a tearoom and cottages.

➏ Keep to the higher path, sometimes over quite rocky ground, to reach the first of the caves. The path continues, climbing again to a second larger cave which lies just off the path. Rejoin the path to enjoy views over Rydal Water and Rydal Fell beyond.

➐ Stay **right** at the wooden bridge and at a fork in the path, dropping down to a wall. Here turn **left** following a sign marked *Grasmere, High Close and Langdale*. At the top of this incline stay **left** (following the blue marker) towards Loughrigg Terrace.

➑ It's here along this narrow curving path that William and Dorothy would stroll, enjoying much the same view over Grasmere, Helm Crag and the higher fells beyond that we enjoy today.

WORDSWORTH'S HOMES

Dove Cottage in Grasmere was known simply as Town End when Wordsworth and his sister moved there at the very end of 1799. Today, in the care of the Wordsworth Trust, the site comprises the original cottage and adjacent Wordsworth Museum and Jerwood Centre, and contains many of his original manuscripts, including the Wordsworth family archive donated to the trust in 1935. Nearby Rydal Mount, the poet's home until his death in 1850, is still in the ownership of the Wordsworth family. Both houses are open to the public.

9 As the path enters woodland go through a metal gate, **forking right** almost immediately through a gate signposted *Grasmere*. This broad path drops down through trees until it reaches Deerbolts Lodge. Here follow the path that swings right in front of the house and drops down gradually to the shore below.

10 At the bottom turn **left** to follow a path along the shoreline. The path stops after a small wooden bridge and climbs left up to some wooden steps and, eventually, a road leading back to Grasmere. Turn **right** and as you reach the village you will pass St Oswald's Church where Wordsworth is buried.

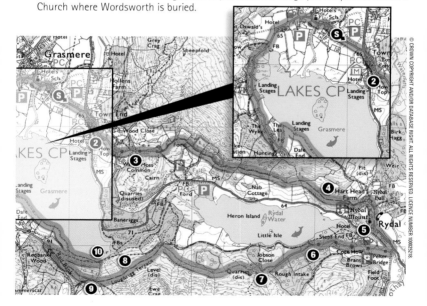

© CROWN COPYRIGHT AND/OR DATABASE RIGHT. ALL RIGHTS RESERVED. LICENCE NUMBER 100025218.

5 GRASMERE & RYDAL WATER

6 Walla Crag & Derwentwater
(John Ruskin) **8.4km/5.2miles**

Lakeland views that art connoisseur considered 'almost too beautiful'.

Keswick • Castle Head • Rakefoot • Walla Crag • Cat Gill • Great Wood • Friar's Crag • Keswick

START
The walk starts in the Lakeside car park, Lake Road (near the Theatre by the Lake), Keswick. GR: NY 265 228.

THE WALK
John Ruskin's artistic stamp can be found all over Europe, but it was the Lake District that left an indelible mark on the man himself.

His home at Brantwood, overlooking Coniston Water and, beyond, the Old Man, is the place today most readily associated with the great Victorian art critic, social commentator, man of letters and learning.

Certainly his spirit lurks in every corner of the house, especially in the dining room where not even the standard of civilised banter may have been enough to distract guests from a view to die for.

But our walk follows Ruskin on his earliest exploration of the Lakes and takes in the view he himself considered one of the finest in Europe.

Derwentwater has never been short of admirers either then or now. Ruskin was just five when his nurse took him to Friar's Crag and, it appears, started a lifelong love affair with the Lakes.

The view over the water towards the Jaws of Borrowdale and Great Gable made a deep impression on the young boy and, arguably, changed the way succeeding generations came to look at the Lake District.

Canon Rawnsley, a founder of the National Trust and a close friend from university days, was largely responsible for the memorial erected there shortly after Ruskin's death in 1900 and it was around Derwentwater that the Trust made its first purchases, among them Friar's Crag itself.

The memorial provides a suitably dramatic finale to our walk which combines ascents of the local beauty spot Castle Head and the more demanding Walla Crag, both summits affording glorious views of the lake and surrounding fells.

Watch out on the return stroll along the lake shore for sculptor Peter Randall-Page's *The Hundred Year Stone*, created to mark the National Trust's 100, year association with this part of Cumbria.

Route finding is straightforward along clear, usually signposted, paths, though the climb to Walla Crag (and the descent afterwards) is steep and, in one or two places, requires care.

DISTANCE: 8.4KM/5.2MILES   **TOTAL ASCENT**: 289M/948FT   **START**: LAKESIDE CAR PARK IN KESWICK (GR: NY 265 228)
TIME: 3 HOURS   **MAP**: OS EXPLORER OL4: THE ENGLISH LAKES (NORTH WESTERN AREA) 1:25,000
REFRESHMENTS: TEAROOM BY LANDING STAGES, PUBS AND RESTAURANTS IN KESWICK   **NAVIGATION**: CLEAR
PATHS AND TRACKS   **SUGGESTED READING**: *ON ART AND LIFE*, JOHN RUSKIN (PUBLISHED BY PENGUIN)

Directions – Walla Crag & Derwentwater

S➔ Turn **left** out of the car park and head towards the lake. At the landing stages (and immediately past the public toilets) take a footpath **left** signposted *Cockshot Wood*. **Ignore** the path running left to right and continue **straight on** through the wood and out across a field at the other side.

2 At the far end of the field climb the steps to the road and cross to enter Castle Head Wood opposite. Climb steeply until the ground levels out near a wooden bench. Some 20 metres after the bench take a footpath running at right angles to the main path. This leads to the summit of Castle Head.

3 **Retrace** your steps to the main path, turn **right** and descend to a kissing gate. The path now leaves the wood and crosses a field to Springs Road. Here turn **right** and follow the road to a stone bridge and stream at the approach to Springs Farm. Follow the stream up through the wood as far as a junction of paths. Turn **right** to follow a path on the edge of the wood.

4 The path eventually rejoins the stream below to cross it at a wooden footbridge. The gate at the other side leads to Castlerigg Road. Here turn **right**, stay **right** where the road forks and cross a second footbridge near Rakefoot to begin an ascent of Walla Crag. Keep the stone wall to your right as the path becomes steeper and curves towards the fell.

5 At a cairn beside a fence turn **right** through a gate to follow a clear, though occasionally hazardous, path along the edge of the crag. **Take particular care on the rocky section above a gully**. The path leads to the summit of Walla Crag from where, on the right day, you will enjoy panoramic views taking in, among others, Blencathra, Skiddaw and Great Gable.

6 Continue on your path, now heading away from the summit to cross the wall at a stile. Head downhill to find a grassy path, keeping the stone wall to your right. This becomes much steeper around Cat Gill. The path eventually drops down into Great Wood and, continuing **straight ahead** by a wooden footbridge, to the National Trust car park.

FRIAR'S CRAG

The Friar's Crag promontory is believed to be the place where monks embarked to make the short journey to St Herbert's Island, the largest of the islands on Derwentwater. St Herbert was a seventh-century priest and confessor who withdrew to the island to devote his life to prayer and mortification and who came to be known as the Hermit of Derwentwater. Wordsworth wrote a poem about St Herbert and his friendship with the better known St Cuthbert of Lindisfarne. The remains of the old hermitage are still visible and mass is celebrated on the island every year in St Herbert's memory.

7 Cross the road and descend by stone steps to a footpath. Turn **left** after 50 metres and follow the path to the lake shore. Continue to follow this path as it winds in and out of the shoreline at Stable Hills but, as the main path heads back towards the road, look out for a gate and yellow waymarked footpath **left** through woods.

8 This leads back to the shore close to the promontory at Friar's Crag. Once through the gate take an **immediate left** to make a short climb to the Ruskin memorial and the now famous view up Derwentwater towards Borrowdale.

9 Turn **right** at the path near the memorial to return to landing stages and the road back to the Lakeside car park.

RUSKIN MEMORIAL AT FRIAR'S CRAG

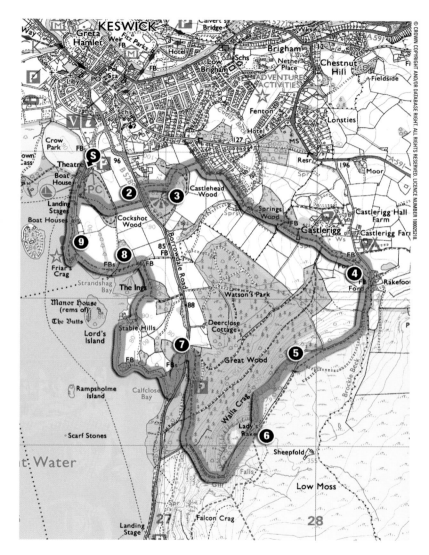

6 WALLA CRAG & DERWENTWATER

The North East, the Moors & the Dales

There's a tremendous range of landscape across Northern England, from the open moors of Northumberland to the rolling Yorkshire Dales and peaty plateaus of the North York Moors. An equally wide-ranging array of literature has drawn on the area, from Stoker's classic horror to Auden's poetry and Herriot's veterinary tales.

HUBBERHOLME AND THE GEORGE INN (ROUTE 12)

SHILDON ENGINE HOUSE (KNOWN LOCALLY AS SHILDON CASTLE)

7 Blanchland
(W. H. Auden)

5.6km/3.5miles

A short walk that pays tribute to an industrial past but also takes in moorland, a river bank and a village loved by two of our most celebrated poets.

Blanchland • Shildon • Pennypie House • Baybridge • Blanchland

START

The walk starts in the public car park at Blanchland which lies south of Hexham on the B6306. There is an honesty box for visitors. GR: NY 964 505.

THE WALK

The Northumberland village of Blanchland has the sort of chocolate box charm that lends itself to TV and cinema.

But poet W. H. Auden saw something else. Auden's love of the North Pennines, expressed in several poems, had more to do with the history of lead mining in the area than it did any aesthetic appeal of the landscape.

He stayed in Blanchland at Easter 1930 and is remembered for a boisterous session on the piano at the local pub. He later confessed that 'no other spot brings me sweeter memories.'

But much of his time was spent visiting local mine workings around the village and imagery of the industry recurs throughout his long poetic career.

Our short walk starts in the centre of the village and passes several disused mine shafts and pit workings, some going back to medieval times.

The most spectacular is Shildon Engine House, built 200 years ago to pump water away from the nearby lead mines. Its remains were conserved in 2010 and today the engine house stands as symbol of a way of life long disappeared.

Auden's abiding fascination for the North Pennines was best recorded in an article that appeared in *American Vogue* in 1954 under the title 'Six Unexpected Days'. Poet Paul Farley recreated the journey for a BBC radio programme in 2007 marking the centenary of the poet's birth.

The village of Blanchland itself is a curious mixture of the industrial and the ecclesiastical. Much of its character derives from the abbey that stood there until 1539.

A few of its buildings also used to be part of the abbey, including St Mary's Church and the Lord Crewe Arms which, as well as hosting Auden, later boasted a connection to the poet Philip Larkin who visited with his long-standing girlfriend Monica Jones.

DISTANCE: 5.6KM/3.5MILES   **TOTAL ASCENT**: 90M/295FT   **START**: PUBLIC CAR PARK IN BLANCHLAND VILLAGE
(GR: NY 964 505)   **TIME**: 2 HOURS   **MAP**: OS EXPLORER OL43: HADRIAN'S WALL, HALTWHISTLE AND HEXHAM
1:25,000   **REFRESHMENTS**: LORD CREWE ARMS, WHITE MONK TEAROOM, BLANCHLAND   **NAVIGATION**:
STRAIGHTFORWARD THROUGHOUT   **SUGGESTED READING**: *COLLECTED POEMS*, W. H. AUDEN (PUBLISHED BY FABER)

Directions – Blanchland

S➔ Turn **right** out of the car park and turn **left almost immediately** and **left again** to follow a public footpath climbing steadily to woods at the back of cottages.

2 **Ignore** the path branching right to continue a climb through trees joining a broad green trail heading right to left. Turn **left** and as the trail descends take a path **right** and then **immediately left** leaving the woods by a small gate.

3 The path now passes at the edge of the wood and continues through a series of bumps and hollows, legacy of the lead mining industry.

4 Pass through a gate and **stay right** to leave the rough pasture by a second gate in front of a cottage. Here **keep left** to follow the track to a lane.

5 Turn **right** (stopping briefly to admire the former mine engine house) and follow the broad stony track as it climbs past disused workings and alongside Shildon Burn towards Pennypie House.

6 **Ignore** the track up to the farm and go forward through a gate onto the moor. Once through the gate turn **immediately left** across a simple bridge to follow a footpath over the moor (signposted *Baybridge*).

7 Follow the path keeping the stone wall to your left. After one kilometre a path joins from the right (leading from a pumping station) and you leave the moor to follow a lane downhill.

8 At the bottom turn **right** on the main road (past a picnic area), briefly crossing the Durham border before turning along a footpath marked *Blanchland and Carrick* (before the bridge).

9 Follow the footpath along the riverside until you reach Blanchland village.

BLANCHLAND

Auden was on a walking tour of Hadrian's Wall when he and his companion Gabriel Carritt stayed at the Lord Crewe Arms in Blanchland. Carritt later recalled being embarrassed by the poet's demands for champagne in the public bar, filled at the time with farm workers. Auden, then 23, rattled out some Brahms on the pub piano and was still fit enough the following morning to suggest a dip in the icy River Derwent.

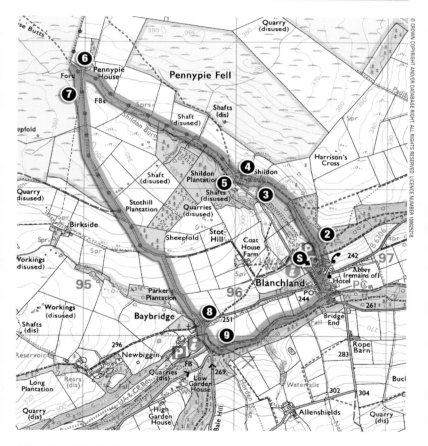

© CROWN COPYRIGHT AND/OR DATABASE RIGHT. ALL RIGHTS RESERVED. LICENCE NUMBER 100025218

7 BLANCHLAND

8 Humbleton Hill & Wooler
(William Shakespeare)

7km/4.3miles

Scenic ascent of a Northumberland hill with a dark history and Shakespearean links.

Wooler • Humbleton • Humbleton Hill • Wooler Common • Wooler

START
Park in public car park opposite St Ninian's Catholic Church in Burnhouse Road, Wooler. GR: NT 989 283.

THE WALK
A large thumb-shaped stone standing in a field just off one of the main roads linking England to Scotland betrays no hint of its bloody history.

The ancient Bendor Stone, outside the Northumberland town of Wooler, serves as unofficial monument to a battle in which the Scots suffered a crushing defeat at the hands of the Earl of Northumberland's forces.

The battle of Homildon Hill in 1402 was decided by the superiority of English bowmen who unleashed a deadly barrage of arrows on their opponents. But the battle is remembered as much for its Shakespearean connections as it is for the part it played in military history.

In *Henry IV Part 1*, the battle is the trigger for a dispute between the monarch and Northumberland's son, Sir Henry Percy (or as he came to be better known 'Harry Hotspur') that ended in the King's victory at the Battle of Shrewsbury.

Homildon Hill is today known as Humbleton Hill and sits just within the boundary of the Northumberland National Park. Our walk starts from Wooler and follows the waymarked trail around the hill and up to the Iron Age hillfort on its summit.

On that steady climb you may well look over to the neighbouring Harehope Hill, where the English archers were positioned, and imagine with a shudder what it was like to be on the receiving end of the hail of arrows that sealed the Scots' fate.

Estimates of battle casualties, then as now, are liable to exaggeration but sources claim that 1,300 Scots lost their lives that day. Shakespeare, never one to allow historical fact to get in the way of a good story, wrote of 'Ten thousand bold Scots, two and twenty knights, Balked in their own blood.'

From the summit there are splendid views of the Milfield Plain and the North Sea beyond. Route finding is straightforward throughout.

DISTANCE: 7KM/4.3MILES **TOTAL ASCENT**: 198M/649FT **START**: BURNHOUSE ROAD CAR PARK IN WOOLER (GR: NT 989 283) **TIME**: ALLOW 2½ HOURS **MAP**: OS EXPLORER OL16: THE CHEVIOT HILLS 1:25000
REFRESHMENTS: PUBS, TEAROOMS AND RESTAURANTS IN WOOLER **NAVIGATION**: STRAIGHTFORWARD THROUGHOUT **SUGGESTED READING**: *HENRY IV PART 1*, WILLIAM SHAKESPEARE (PUBLISHED BY OXFORD PAPERBACKS)

Directions – Humbleton Hill & Wooler

S Turn **left** out of the car park along Burnhouse Road, passing Highburn House caravan park after half a mile.

2 Immediately after the caravan park turn **left** over a stone bridge on a public footpath marked *Humbleton*. Cross the field on a clear track.

3 Pass through two gates, the second of which leads to a lane. Here turn **left** and make gentle ascent to the hamlet of Humbleton.

4 Turn **left** at the T junction (next to a telephone box) and continue past houses and through a gate. Turn **right** on a bridleway signposted *Gleadscleugh*, cross the stile and continue on a clear grassy path with ponds to your right.

5 **Bear left** off the bridleway following yellow footpath signs alongside a fence. Cross the stile and continue on the grassy path which skirts Humbleton Hill climbing all the while.

6 The path forks left about 20 metres before a gate and climbs more steeply to a stile over an (electrified) fence. Continue along the path to the remains of the hillfort at the summit.

7 From the cairn **retrace** your steps for a few paces until there is a clear break in the wall and a grassy path leading down. Follow this to a gate half a mile distant at the foot of the hill.

8 Turn **right** and follow the bridleway to a gate, keeping the stone wall on your right. Shortly after the gate turn **left** through a second gate and follow the path towards woods.

9 Go through the gate at entrance to the woods and descend to Wooler Common on a fairly steep woodland track. As you emerge from the wood turn **left** along metalled footpath above Humbleton Burn.

HARRY HOTSPUR

Sir Henry Percy may have come to a sticky end at the Battle of Shrewsbury but, thanks to Shakespeare, he cuts a dashing figure to this day – and one who is remembered in the unlikeliest of places. Percy – or Harry Hotspur – came from Alnwick and made his name in a series of battles with raiding Scots armies. Having helped Henry IV to the throne, he fell from favour and found himself on the wrong side of history at Shrewsbury. The Percy family owned land on Tottenham Marshes and gave the name Hotspur to a certain London football club.

❿ As the path swings right continue **straight** on a grassy path which eventually crosses the burn and leads to Common Road. Here turn **left** and follow back into Wooler. As you reach High Street turn **left** to return to Burnhouse Road.

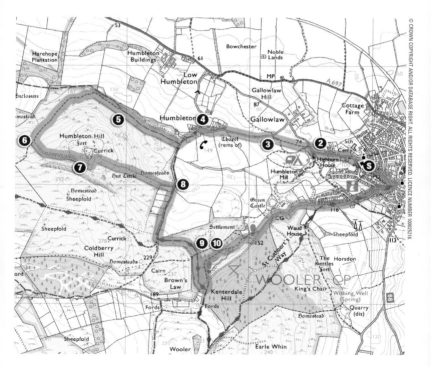

© CROWN COPYRIGHT AND/OR DATABASE RIGHT. ALL RIGHTS RESERVED. LICENCE NUMBER 100025218.

8 HUMBLETON HILL & WOOLER

9 Cleadon Hills & Marsden Rock
(Catherine Cookson)

10.5km/6.5miles

A walk through a landscape in change, taking in the natural beauty of Marsden Rock and the man-made splendour of Souter Lighthouse.

Whitburn • Cleadon Hills • Marsden Old Quarry • Marsden Rock • Souter Lighthouse • Whitburn

START

The walk starts in the seafront car park at Whitburn Bents on the A183 between Sunderland and South Shields.
GR: NZ 408 613.

THE WALK

Memories of Catherine Cookson, once a giant of popular fiction, are fading. Even on Tyneside where she grew up and from which she drew much of her inspiration, Cookson's name is no longer seen as a magnet for visitors.

This is a shame. Few writers are as closely associated with a particular place as the romantic novelist whose books sold more than 100 million copies and who at one time (and not so long ago) was the UK's most widely read author.

Today you still see the area around South Shields described on old information boards as 'Catherine Cookson Country' but the commemorative walking trail has disappeared along with her mass appeal.

Our walk doesn't attempt to incorporate every landmark from Cookson's life and fiction – there are too many – but instead gives a taste of the way the landscape populated by her characters has interacted with the industry from which, by and large, they eked out a modest living.

The gentlest of ascents from the village of Whitburn to the highest point on the Cleadon Hills affords views down the coastline south towards Whitby. But the centrepiece of the walk is a stroll along the coastal path and, effectively, through the social history of this part of South Shields.

Marsden Rock, a 100-foot-high stack of magnesian limestone, features several times in Cookson's fiction, notably in *Mrs Flannagan's Trumpet*, published in 1989. The rock, like much of the immediate coast-line, is now owned by the National Trust and is subject to fairly dramatic erosion.

Nor is it just the cliffs that have changed around here. When Marsden Colliery was in operation a thriving community of 135 homes, a school, chapel and Co-op grew up on the cliff top, only to be demolished in 1968 when the pit and nearby limekiln closed for the last time. Route finding is straightforward throughout though paths along field edges can be muddy.

DISTANCE: 10.5KM/6.5MILES **TOTAL ASCENT**: 80M/262FT **START**: WHITBURN BENTS CAR PARK (GR: NZ 408 613) **TIME**: 3 HOURS **MAP**: OS EXPLORER 316: NEWCASTLE UPON TYNE 1:25,000 **REFRESHMENTS**: LATIMERS'S SEAFOOD DELI AND CAFÉ NEAR CAR PARK AND PUBS AND RESTAURANTS IN WHITBURN **NAVIGATION**: STRAIGHTFORWARD THROUGHOUT, SOME ROAD WALKING AT OUTSET **SUGGESTED READING**: MRS FLANNAGAN'S TRUMPET, CATHERINE COOKSON (PUBLISHED BY PICCOLO)

Directions – Cleadon Hills & Marsden Rock

S Cross Coast Road and aim **diagonally right** across Cornthwaite Park to emerge on Church Lane near the parish church. Continue towards the main road and **cross with care**. Turn **left** and then **right** up Sandy Chare.

2 Pass the village pond and old schoolhouse on the left and continue **straight ahead** up Wellands Lane (houses on both sides) for half a mile.

3 Turn **left** along a public footpath towards Well House Farm. At the farm continue **straight ahead** until the path swings right to begin a gentle ascent of Cleadon Hills through a series of stiles. At the highest point there are views of Sunderland's football stadium and, down the coast, of the Cleveland Hills and Whitby.

4 The path eventually emerges at a nature reserve close to Cleadon Windmill. From the mill follow the path alongside a stone wall and through a kissing gate, passing a water pumping station on your left.

5 A green metal gate in a high fence gives access to a golf course. Cross the course taking care to follow the yellow markers and keep an eye out for stray shots.

6 Leave the golf course by a stile in a stone wall and turn immediately **right** to follow the wall until the path finally emerges at a main road close to a caravan site. Cross the road and follow a footpath between the caravan park and the golf course to reach the coast road.

7 **Cross** the road to the metal railings that guard the cliff edge. After enjoying the view of Marsden Rock turn **right** and follow the coastal path along a spectacular stretch of coastline which is under constant threat of erosion and which contains several reminders of its industrial past. **Take care to stay the right side of the railings** and to observe any local safety instructions.

8 The path passes the magnificent Souter Lighthouse, built in 1871 and the first lighthouse to be powered by electricity. Shortly after passing Whitburn rifle ranges you will see the car park where you started your walk.

CLEADON

At the age of 18 Catherine Cookson got a job in the laundry at Harton Moor workhouse in South Shields, occasionally visiting the Cottage Homes at Cleadon where poor children were looked after in 'family' groups. The cottages, built to house and provide vocational education for children who were orphaned or otherwise needed care, had a reputation for no-nonsense discipline, something not immediately obvious from their flowery names – Primrose, Violet, Daisy and Snowdrop among them.

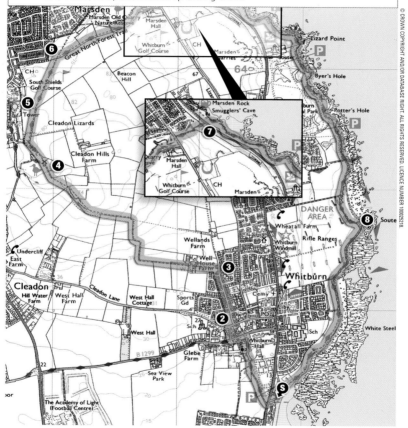

© CROWN COPYRIGHT AND/OR DATABASE RIGHT. ALL RIGHTS RESERVED. LICENCE NUMBER 100025218.

9 CLEADON HILLS & MARSDEN ROCK

WHITBY ABBEY

10 Whitby
(Bram Stoker)

9.5km/6miles

A dramatic coastal walk taking in one of Yorkshire's most famous landmarks.

Whitby Abbey • Cleveland Way • Bram Stoker Memorial Seat • 199 Steps • Whitby Abbey

START
Park in the car park at Whitby Abbey, Abbey Lane. GR: NZ 904 109.

THE WALK
The fishing village of Whitby has long been a popular destination for holidaymakers. But it's fair to say that when Abraham 'Bram' Stoker came here looking for a suitable location for a family break back in 1890 he saw a place no-one had ever quite seen before.

Stoker's visit to Whitby – especially the dramatic coastal setting of its abbey – fired an imagination nurtured on tales of East European folklore and its fascination with vampires.

The story goes that he booked himself into the Royal Hotel and began work immediately on the character the world now knows as Dracula. We know that he carried out some research at Whitby library and for better or worse the Yorkshire resort is now seemingly inextricably linked to the most famous vampire of all.

Stoker, originally a theatre critic from Dublin, had married and moved to London where he took up the post of business manager at the Lyceum Theatre.

Mixing with some of most famous actors and writers of his time – among them Sir Arthur Conan Doyle, W.B. Yeats and Oscar Wilde – it was no surprise that he himself began writing.

But his life took a different course after meeting the Hungarian writer and traveller Armin Vambery. It was Vambery who inspired Stoker to explore folklore and, in particular, its dark fascination with the living dead.

In Stoker's imagination, the Russian schooner 'The Demeter' is washed up in Whitby harbour following a wild storm, its captain and crew all dead. The only survivor is a huge black dog seen to leap from the boat and bound up the 199 steps to Whitby Abbey.

We now know, of course, that a dog is just one of the many forms a vampire can take. Dracula had arrived in England!

DISTANCE: 9.5KM/6MILES   **TOTAL ASCENT**: 60M/196FT   **START**: WHITBY ABBEY CAR PARK (GR: NZ 904 109)
TIME: 2½ HOURS   **MAP**: OS EXPLORER OL27: NORTH YORK MOORS (EASTERN AREA) 1:25,000
REFRESHMENTS: PUBS AND TEAROOMS IN WHITBY AND AT THE WHITBY YHA   **NAVIGATION**: CLEAR COASTAL
PATHS AND COUNTRYSIDE TRACKS: CHECK WEATHER AS COASTAL PATH MAY CLOSE IN ADVERSE CONDITIONS
SUGGESTED READING: *DRACULA*, BRAM STOKER (PUBLISHED BY WORDSWORTH CLASSICS)

Directions – Whitby

S➤ From the car park, return to the main road and turn **left** following the path signposted *Headland and St Mary's Church*. Continue around the perimeter of the Abbey until you reach three stone archways. Cross the road and take the public footpath signposted *Cleveland Way and Robin Hood's Bay 6.5 miles*.

2 Follow the coastal path until you descend some stone steps passing a National Trust sign for *Salwich Nab*. Follow the path through the caravan park to the right and at the end of the site **take the road curving to the right** (**ignoring** the signs for Salwich Bay and Robin Hood's Bay).

3 Turn **right** at the first waymark sign you see (opposite a telegraph pole) and follow the path along the edge of a field, keeping to the path to cross two further fields until you reach a wooden stile.

4 Cross the stile, then cross the road turning **left** to walk along a path by a wall. Turn **right** at a sign for public footpath at the side of a field. Through a kissing gate walk past farm buildings and continue **straight on**. **Ignore** the path as it swings to the right and continue down a small dirt track to the **left** that turns into a flagged footpath.

5 Continue until you cross the main road, following The Ropery round and descending a steep cobbled slope to the **left** to reach Quay Street. Turn **right** and then **cross** the road, turning **left** after the car park and **immediate left** to pass the Captain Cook Memorial Museum on Grape Lane.

6 At the top of Grape Lane take an immediate **left** to cross Whitby Bridge and turn **right** to walk along the Quayside. Turn **left** at the RNLI Whitby Lifeboat Museum and follow the winding path to reach some steps on the **left**. Here you will find the Bram Stoker memorial seat and can admire the view of the Abbey that inspired him.

7 **Go back down** the steps and follow the path around East Terrace until you reach the Whalebone Arch. Follow the steps down and return along the Quayside and cross Whitby Bridge.

199 STEPS

Whitby's 199 steps are central to the *Dracula* story. When Mina saw her friend Lucy being attacked by the vampire – 'something long and black, bending over the half-reclining white figure' – she raced up the steps to the churchyard in an attempt to save her. Of course, by the time she got there Dracula had fled the scene. Writer and church lover Simon Jenkins has described the climb as 'the most exhilarating approach to any church in England.'

❽ Take an **immediate left** turn up Sandgate, then **right** passing the Shambles market, and finally **left** up Church Lane. You return to the car park via the 199 steps to Whitby Abbey.

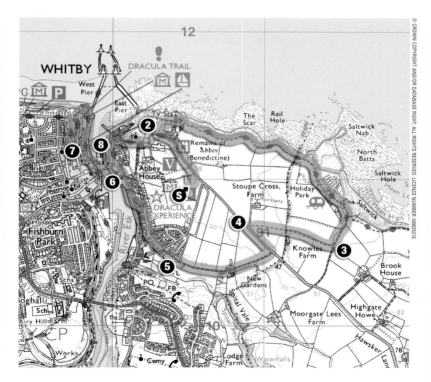

© CROWN COPYRIGHT AND/OR DATABASE RIGHT. ALL RIGHTS RESERVED. LICENCE NUMBER 100023218.

10 WHITBY

11 Around Thirsk
(James Herriot)

In and around the market town where fact met fiction for popular vet.

Sowerby • Blakey Bridge • New Bridge • Old Thirsk • New Thirsk • Sowerby

START
Park on road near the Methodist Church in Front Street, Sowerby.
GR: SE 430 813.

THE WALK
They were books that inspired a generation to try its hand at veterinary science, spawned a television series that made us nostalgic for the '30s, and brought the North Yorkshire countryside to a worldwide audience.

Alf Wight may or not have been the best vet ever to have thrust his arm up a cow's backside but as James Herriot he gave the profession a feel-good factor it retains to this day.

As the main character in the series of books that began with *If Only They Could Talk*, published in 1970, Herriot started work as a raw veterinary assistant at a practice that served a distinctive breed of surly, tight-fisted Dales farmers.

The fictional practice was based in Darrowby, recognisable as the real-life market town of Thirsk.

Wight, originally from Sunderland, was a young child when his family moved to Glasgow. He remained there until 1939 when he qualified as a vet from Glasgow Veterinary College.

After successfully applying for the position of veterinary assistant in Thirsk, he stayed with the practice for 50 years, preferring rural life to the hustle and bustle of the big city.

But Wight was also an affectionate observer of the people and animals he worked with.

His characters – grumpy farmers, idiosyncratic vets and even the infamously plump Pekingese Tricky Woo – were all larger than life and were one reason why the books lent themselves so readily to adaptation by TV (in the BBC series *All Creatures Great and Small*) and cinema.

But, of course, there was another natural performer in the magnificent countryside around Thirsk. Our walk starts in Sowerby, continues into Thirsk, passing Wight's home – now 'The World of James Herriot', a museum dedicated to the fictional vet.

DISTANCE: 8KM/5MILES **TOTAL ASCENT**: 20M/66FT **START**: METHODIST CHURCH, FRONT STREET, SOWERBY, ON ROAD PARKING PERMITTED (GR: SE 430 813) **TIME**: 2½ HOURS **MAP**: OS EXPLORER 302: NORTHALLERTON AND THIRSK, 1:25,000 **REFRESHMENTS**: TEAROOMS AND PUBS IN THIRSK **NAVIGATION**: FLAT, CLEAR PATHS THROUGH VILLAGE AND FIELDS **SUGGESTED READING**: *IF ONLY THEY COULD TALK* AND *IT SHOULDN'T HAPPEN TO A VET*, JAMES HERRIOT (PUBLISHED BY PAN)

Directions – Around Thirsk

S→ From the Methodist Church walk down Front Street a short distance and turn **left** down Blakey Lane, following the off road footpath to the left. Cross a stone bridge and take an **immediate left** to follow a path through a field passing through a series of kissing gates.

❷ Continue with the stream to your left and pass through a stile and two gates before reaching a petrol station on the main road. Cross the road and follow the public footpath by the side of the bridge with a brick wall to your right. Continue **straight on** passing a village green until you reach a main road.

❸ At the Lord Nelson pub **cross** the road and follow the footpath to the **left**. Where the road curves to the right, follow the path that runs to the **left** past some houses. By the final house, follow the footpath crossing a metal bridge and continue **straight on** with Cod Beck running to your right.

❹ Just before you reach a main road take the path to the **right** past a children's play area. Cross a footbridge, pass through two gates and follow the path as it runs alongside the river.

❺ Cross a stile and then a second stile on the right. Continue across two more stiles. As you approach some mill buildings cross the footbridge to the **left** and continue to **follow the path** as it curves to cross a second bridge on the left.

❻ Turn **right** onto a bridleway, pass through a gate and **bear left** to cross a field to meet a main road. Turn **left** out of the field and walk for about 20 metres before crossing the road and passing through a large gap in the hedge marked by a waymark. Follow the path until you reach a gate by a wooded area.

❼ Go through the gate and continue **straight on** with the woodland to your left. About 120 metres past the woodland turn **left** through a waymarked gap in the hedge. Continue **straight on** passing through two fields. In the second field cross a stile on the **left**, walking with the hedge to your right until you reach and cross a second stile.

23 KIRKGATE, THIRSK

Alf Wight's old veterinary practice at 23 Kirkgate, Thirsk, is now a popular museum, which gives fans of his books (and schoolchildren not yet born when he died in 1995) an insight into the old ways of animal medicine. The James Herriot Museum boasts an impressive range of saws and other implements used by vets in their day to day business in the surgery and out on the hills. There's also a fine array of bottles which, in the days before antibiotics, produced the secret potions and mixtures on which a vet's reputation rested.

8 Walk across the field **bearing left** until you reach a grass track running between hedgerows. Continue **straight on** passing allotments and a graveyard on the right. As you leave the path continue **straight on** and follow the road as it bears left, with a brick wall on the left, and then bears right passing St Mary's Church.

9 Turn **right** and continue **straight on**, passing James Herriot's fictional house (marked by a blue heritage plaque), into Market Place. Turn **right** and follow the road as it curves left, then right. At a mini roundabout take the road to the **left** (Sowerby Road).

10 Continue along Sowerby Road to Front Street and the point where the walk began.

ST MARY'S CHURCH, THIRSK

ALF WIGHT'S FORMER HOUSE – NOW THE HERRIOT MUSEUM

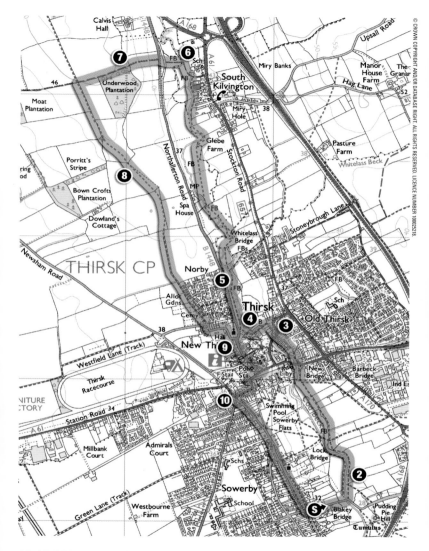

11 AROUND THIRSK

© CROWN COPYRIGHT AND/OR DATABASE RIGHT. ALL RIGHTS RESERVED. LICENCE NUMBER 100025318.

HUBBERHOLME – THE LONG VIEW

12 Upper Wharfedale & Hubberholme
(J. B. Priestley)

7km/4.5miles

Round the rim of one of Upper Wharfedale's most scenic valleys and through the village loved by this popular writer.

Buckden • Cray • Scar House • Hubberholme • Buckden

START
The walk starts in the village of Buckden on the B6160 at the Yorkshire Dales National Park car park. GR: SD 942 773.

THE WALK
Writer J. B. Priestley knew England in the '30s better than most. So when he describes the Dales village of Hubberholme as 'one of the smallest and pleasantest places in the world' he was speaking out of more than just native Yorkshire pride.

His book *English Journey* took him to all four corners of the country in the period between the wars and is still considered a thoughtful and sympathetic account of working life. No less a name than George Orwell drew inspiration from the book when he embarked on his own subsequent journey across England, described in *The Road to Wigan Pier*.

But if it is Priestley's descriptions of towns and cities which stick in the memory there is not much doubt where the author's own affections lay.

Priestley wanted his ashes scattered in Hubberholme, the halfway point on this walk, and it is in the church and in the George Inn, his favourite pub, that he is best remembered.

A plaque in the Church of St Michael and All Angels is the most visible reminder of Priestley's connection with the village, but his love of the English countryside is crystallised in the hills around.

It's easy to see the appeal. Our walk contains the very essence of Upper Wharfedale – a limestone landscape where change arrives at glacial pace.

The hard bit comes early – a steep climb out of Buckden brings sweat to the brow. But route finding is straightforward and the views spectacular. On the right day you will see the village church poking through trees and the white walls of the George Inn from a long way off.

Take care on the equally steep descent into Cray, particularly in wet weather. Above Cray there is a splendid limestone pavement which affords magnificent views down the valley and which must rank as one of the finest spots in Yorkshire for 'elevenses.'

DISTANCE: 7KM/4.5MILES **TOTAL ASCENT**: 137M, 450FT **START**: CAR PARK IN BUCKDEN (GR: SD 942 773)
TIME: 2 HOURS **MAP**: OS EXPLORER OL30: YORKSHIRE DALES (NORTHERN AND CENTRAL AREAS) 1:25,000
REFRESHMENTS: PUBS IN CRAY, HUBBERHOLME AND BUCKDEN, TEAROOM IN BUCKDEN **NAVIGATION**: CLEAR PATHS
AND TRACKS **SUGGESTED READING**: *ENGLISH JOURNEY*, J. B. PRIESTLEY (PUBLISHED BY GREAT NORTHERN BOOKS)

Directions – Upper Wharfedale & Hubberholme

S Leave the car park by a gate at the northern end and follow a bridleway signposted *Buckden Pike* and *Cray High Bridge*, climbing steadily above the valley. As you gain height there is a first glimpse through the trees of the church tower at Hubberholme.

2 As the track levels out keep the drystone wall to your left, **ignoring** a footpath sign to Buckden Pike. Where the wall ends continue **forward** on a grassy track for a short while until another wall emerges on your left.

3 After 500 metres turn **left** at a signpost for *Cray*, dropping down steeply at first over a rocky path. Cross Cray Gill at stepping stones to reach the White Lion car park opposite.

4 Cross the road and take the track to the **right** of the pub, staying right to pass through a farmyard. Continue through gates and past barns to emerge on a stony track through fields.

5 Continue forward on a clear track, following the path as it drops down to cross Crook Gill at a wooden footbridge built by volunteers. **Bear left** at the other side and take time to admire the views of the valley floor from the limestone pavement.

6 From time to time you will see some remarkable limestone formations underfoot – strangely reminiscent of works by the Yorkshire sculptor Henry Moore. The path narrows as you pass woodland on your left, enclosed by a mossy wall.

7 Above Scar House follow the signpost marked *Hubberholme* (**ignoring** one to *Yockenthwaite*) and drop down behind the house to pick up a metalled road leading to the village.

8 The church of St Michael and All Angels greets walkers at the approach to the tiny village. Over the bridge turn **left** in front of the George Inn and follow the road for about a quarter of a mile to a signpost marked *Buckden Bridge (part of the Dales Way)*.

9 Turn **left** here to follow the river back to the bridge below the village of Buckden. At that bridge turn **left** and follow the road back to the village centre and car park.

ENGLISH JOURNEY

J. B. Priestley identified three different Englands on his 1934 journey from north to south and east to west. He described Old England as the country of cathedrals and minsters, and manor houses and inns, 19th-century England as an industrial landscape of dismal towns and fortress-like cities, and the new post-war England as a place of dance halls and cafés where everything was given away for cigarette coupons. He claimed the City had done to the industrial North 'what the black-moustached glossy gentleman in the old melodrama always did to the innocent village maiden.'

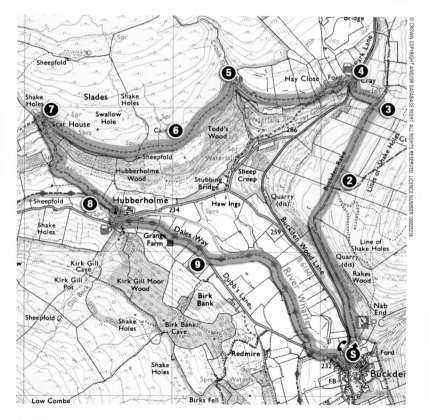

© CROWN COPYRIGHT AND/OR DATABASE RIGHT ALL RIGHTS RESERVED. LICENCE NUMBER 100025218.

12 UPPER WHARFEDALE & HUBBERHOLME

JANET'S FOSS

13 Malham Tarn & Cove
(Charles Kingsley)

Charles Kingsley imagines a world of steepling cliffs, magical waterfalls and bleak moorland – features immediately recognisable on this circular walk.

Malham • Janet's Foss • Gordale Scar • Street Gate • Malham Tarn • Tarn House • Malham Cove • Malham

START
The walk starts in the centre of Malham at the Yorkshire Dales National Park car park. GR: SD 900 626.

THE WALK
Victorian writer Charles Kingsley stayed at Tarn House, overlooking Malham Tarn, in the heart of Yorkshire's limestone country in 1858. We know that he used the countryside around as inspiration for *The Water Babies*, published five years later and still the book for which he is best known.

It is a children's book which tells the story of a young chimney sweep who, on the run from a bullying employer, makes a hair-raising descent of a fictional Malham Cove, flees across moorland, finally finding refuge in a village modelled on the real-life Arncliffe.

The book's most memorable scenes take place in a stream where our hero Tom swims with fairies and emerges – cleansed – to a new life. Though written for children, it picks up some of Kingsley's favourite themes, among them the plight of the Victorian poor and the awful sanitary conditions they faced.

Malhamdale's spectacular natural features continue to attract visitors from all the over the world and the first section of the walk – as far as Gordale Scar – can be a procession at weekends. But the magical atmosphere of Janet's Foss, by legend the home of a fairy queen, is somehow unspoiled by the tramp of walkers come to enjoy one of the most popular sights in the Dales.

Above Gordale, however, the landscape is wilder and provides fine contrast to the picture postcard appeal of the tourist hotspots.

There is also a short detour to Tarn House, former home of the Morrison family where Kingsley stayed during his time in Malham. The building is today used as field centre where a variety of arts and natural history courses are taught *(NB. It is not open to the public)*.

Some of the paths on the walk are accessible to wheelchairs and pushchairs. At other points, however, great care is needed, especially when crossing the limestone pavement at the top of Malham Cove.

DISTANCE: 14.7KM/9.1MILES   **TOTAL ASCENT**: 194M/639FT   **START**: YORKSHIRE DALES NATIONAL PARK CAR PARK, MALHAM (GR: SD 900 626)   **TIME**: ALLOW 3½ HOURS   **MAP**: OS EXPLORER OL2: YORKSHIRE DALES (SOUTHERN AND WESTERN AREAS) 1:25,000   **REFRESHMENTS**: BUCK INN AND LISTER ARMS IN MALHAM, OLD BARN TEAROOM
NAVIGATION: CLEAR PATHS AND TRACKS, CARE NEEDED WHEN WALKING ON LIMESTONE IN WET WEATHER
SUGGESTED READING: *THE WATER BABIES*, CHARLES KINGSLEY (PUBLISHED BY WORDSWORTH CHILDREN'S CLASSICS)

Directions – Malham Tarn & Cove

S➨ Turn **left** out of the car park and cross the beck at the bridge behind Malham Smithy. Turn **right** to follow the popular and well-signposted path, eventually passing through woods, to Janet's Foss.

2 Follow the path **left** from the waterfall to the road. Here turn **right** crossing two adjacent bridges over Gordale Beck and, for the time being at least, **ignoring** the footpath left over fields to Malham Cove. Instead leave the road at a bend, following the footpath **left** through a camp site to Gordale Scar.

3 The spectacle that awaits as the footpath curves right has entranced artists for centuries. Enjoy the view, taking account of conditions on the day and general fitness and agility, decide which of two routes to take to reach Street Gate.

4 To take the direct route cross the stream and climb to the **left** of the waterfall, taking care on slippery rock. The short scramble leads to a stepped path and eventually a grassy track that leads to Street Gate.

OR➨ Optional route:
Otherwise **retrace** your steps to the footpath sign to Malham Cove ignored at Step 2 and climb the field joining the wall on your right. Pass through two gates, the second of which is situated in the top right hand corner of the field, and turn **left** alongside another wall. Keeping the wall to your left this well-defined path eventually leads to a lane. Follow the lane as it winds uphill for about a mile to a cattle grid. Shortly after the cattle grid there is a footpath sign on the **right** leading back to Gordale Scar – an optional diversion – and a little way beyond that a clear track bearing right to Street Gate.

5 At the junction continue along the path signposted *Arncliffe*, forking **left** on a grassy path immediately after the cattle grid. When you reach the clearly defined path close to Malham Tarn turn **right** and follow it through woods to Tarn House (not open to the public).

TARN HOUSE

Charles Kingsley's host at Tarn House was Walter Morrison, millionaire businessman, bachelor, patron of the arts and proud (adopted) Yorkshireman. Morrison inherited the house on his father's death in 1857 and thereafter opened the doors not just to some of the leading figures of his day – among them John Ruskin, Charles Darwin and John Stuart Mill - but also to what the editor of *The Times* called 'bean feasters of every description.' His generosity lives on today in the Gothic chapel and famous copper dome at nearby Giggleswick School, paid for by Morrison to commemorate Queen Victoria's Diamond Jubilee.

6 **Retrace** your steps back to the shore of the tarn keeping **right** until you reach a gate beside a plantation. Bear **right** immediately afterwards at a signpost marked *Pennine Way* and follow to a road near a car park.

7 Over the stream go through a gate on your **left** and fork **left** at the footpath marked *Malham Cove*. This skirts the hill, eventually emerging to a dramatic view from the head of Watlowes.

8 Cross the stile and begin a steepish descent over rough steps keeping the wall on your left. Leave Ewe Moor through a gated stile and as a popular footpath joins from the left turn **right** over the magnificent limestone pavement at the top of Malham Cove.

9 At the other side of the pavement there is a footpath that goes through a gate and then begins a stepped descent. At the bottom **keep left** and follow the stream to the foot of the cove.

10 Retrace your steps keeping the stream on your **left** until you reach a small stone bridge. Cross here and at the other side climb to a footpath which heads through fields towards Malham. Passing the youth hostel on your left you will enter the village by the Lister Arms. Turn **right** and follow the road over the bridge back to the car park.

LIMESTONE PAVEMENT AT MALHAM COVE

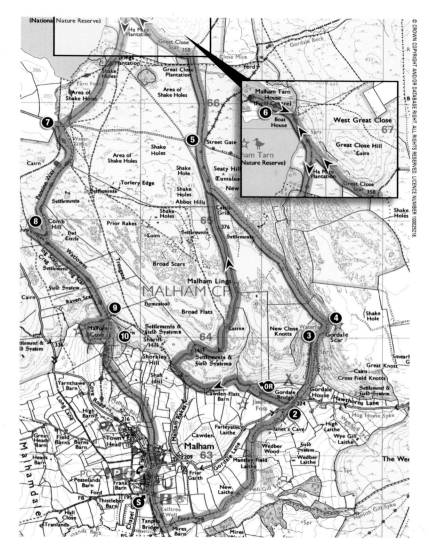

13 MALHAM TARN & COVE

© CROWN COPYRIGHT AND/OR DATABASE RIGHT. ALL RIGHTS RESERVED. LICENCE NUMBER 100028218.

Peak District, South Pennines & Cheshire

The area around Derbyshire's Peak District is one of the UK's most popular walking regions. Fitting then, that some of the country's most beloved literature – from the Brontës, Tolkien and Carroll – drew inspiration from the area.

APPROACH TO BRONTË WATERFALL (ROUTE 15)

OLD HODDER BRIDGE (OR CROMWELL'S BRIDGE)

14 Hurst Green & Stonyhurst College
(J. R. R. Tolkien)

10.5km/6.5miles

Through fields and woodland around the famous Catholic college where Tolkien wrote part of his classic adventure.

Hurst Green • Winkley Hall • Lower Hodder Bridge • Stonyhurst College • Hurst Green

START

The walk starts in the village of Hurst Green. Parking in the village hall car park. GR: SD 684 382.

THE WALK

Quite a few places claim to have been the inspiration for Middle Earth, the mythical land brought so vividly to life by J. R. R. Tolkien in his trilogy *The Lord of the Rings*.

But those familiar with the area around Stonyhurst College in Lancashire's Ribble Valley entertain no doubts about the countryside Tolkien had in mind when he put pen to paper for that classic of children's literature.

Tolkien, then a professor at Oxford University, stayed at Stonyhurst several times between 1942 and 1947 and is said to have written parts of his epic trilogy in a classroom at the college to which his son John had been evacuated. Father and son are said to have spent many hours walking the fields and woods around.

Literary detectives point to some of the similarities between local names and those chosen by Tolkien for his fictional landscape. There is a Shire Lane in the village of Hurst Green where our walk starts and it seems likely that the imaginary River Shirebourn has its linguistic roots in the name of the Shireburn family which built Stonyhurst.

This area is also, in some people's eyes, close to the geographical centre of Great Britain, thereby providing some scientific backing for its claims to have inspired Middle Earth.

But, detective or no, the walker in these parts will find echoes of the Tolkien fantasy everywhere. Over the course of six and a bit miles there are distant hills, three rivers, a now disused ferry crossing, some magical patches of woodland and, in Hurst Green, a quintessential English village.

The final stretch also passes St Mary's Hall, now a preparatory school to the main college where Tolkien's youngest son Michael taught in the late 1960s and early 1970s.

Route finding is straightforward throughout, but the going can be heavy underfoot.

DISTANCE: 10.5KM/6.5MILES   **TOTAL ASCENT**: 137M/450FT   **START**: HURST GREEN VILLAGE HALL CAR PARK
(GR: SD 684 382)   **TIME**: 3 HOURS   **MAP**: OS EXPLORER 287: WEST PENNINE MOORS 1:25,000   **REFRESHMENTS**: THREE
PUBS IN HURST GREEN   **NAVIGATION**: ROUTE FINDING STRAIGHTFORWARD BUT CAN BE MUDDY UNDERFOOT
SUGGESTED READING: *THE LORD OF THE RINGS*, J. R. R. TOLKIEN (PUBLISHED BY HARPER COLLINS)

Directions – Hurst Green & Stonyhurst College

S→ Turn **left** out of the car park down the village towards the Shireburn Arms pub. Take the path to the **left of the pub** and follow through a gate down a field with a stream to your left. Across a wooden bridge turn **left** to find a stile and path leading down to a second bridge and eventually the River Ribble. Pendle Hill, a companion for much of the walk, looms in the distance.

2 Bear **left** heading for an aqueduct. Cross a stile to the left of the aqueduct and continue to follow the river bank eventually joining a metalled road. Leave the road at a wooden stile just beyond a small stone building and follow a footpath along the bend of the river.

3 **Continue** to follow a clear path alongside the river. The magnificently mullioned Hacking Hall on the opposite bank marks the confluence of the rivers Ribble and Calder and the spot where, in Tolkien's time, the Hacking Ferry would provide passage for locals.

4 **Continue** along the river bank to the point where the rivers Ribble and Hodder join. Here pass a wooden bench on your right to go through a marked gate **straight ahead**. This eventually leads through Winkley Hall Farm.

5 At the other side of the farm the broad track climbs towards Winkley Hall. As the track swings left turn **right** through a metal kissing gate into a field. Here you will get your first glimpse of the distinctive towers of Stonyhurst College. Cross the field to a second kissing gate and then **veer slightly right** to follow a path on the edge of woodland. This leads to down to a main road.

6 Turn **right** at the road and follow the pavement as far as Lower Hodder Bridge. Here you can make a short detour right for a view of the Old Hodder Bridge, otherwise known as Cromwell's Bridge. After the detour return to the main road and **cross with care** to take a track immediately **left** before the bridge.

7 Follow the track with the river to your right until it passes Hodder Place, once the home of a wealthy mill owner, and eventually descends to a stone bridge. At the other side of the bridge turn immediately **left** alongside a stream to reach a wooden footbridge and a formidable flight of steps.

STONYHURST COLLEGE

Tolkien's son John was studying for the priesthood at the English College in Rome when he was evacuated to the Jesuit seminary at St Mary's Hall, now the college's preparatory school. The family visited regularly, staying at a guest house in the grounds, and Tolkien himself occasionally taught at the main college. The connection continued when Michael, the younger son, taught classics at Stonyhurst in the 1960s and early 1970s. A Tolkien library was opened at St Mary's Hall in 2002.

8 At the top, cross a stile **left** into a field and keep to the edge of the field until a second stile gives access to a broad stone track. **Keep left** until you reach the main road. Cross the road and take the path (almost immediately opposite) to the left of a post box.

9 The track keeps to the left of a hedge bordering St Mary's Hall and passes playing fields and college buildings. As the tarmac track swings right towards the main college turn **left** through a gate at the end of a wall. The path eventually drops down to the edge of a wood before climbing to a kissing gate. Cross and follow the track through two gates to reach a narrow lane. Turn **left** and follow the lane until it joins the village close to the village hall.

STONYHURST COLLEGE

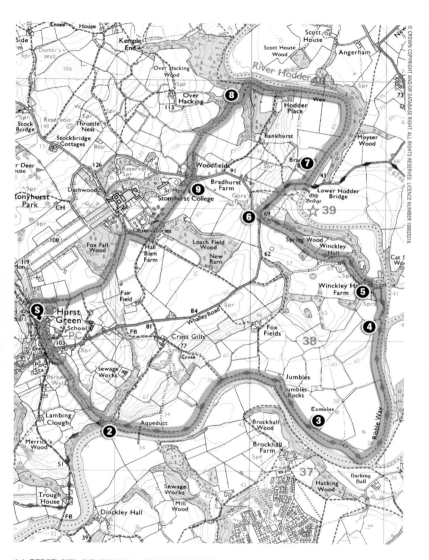

14 HURST GREEN & STONYHURST COLLEGE

© CROWN COPYRIGHT AND/OR DATABASE RIGHT. ALL RIGHTS RESERVED. LICENCE NUMBER 100025218.

15 Haworth & the Moors
(The Brontë sisters)

A walk on the wuthering side.

Haworth • Brontë Waterfall • Haworth Moor • Top Withens • Stanbury • Haworth

START

The walk starts at Haworth railway station, Station Road, Haworth. GR: SE 034 372.

THE WALK

Considering their lives were short, unglamorous, and largely played out in a then remote corner of Yorkshire, the impact of the Brontë sisters on our culture has been immense.

Rarely a year goes by without some new TV or film adaptation of their stories, a fact which in part explains the global nature of their appeal. These days even the signposts around Haworth come with a Japanese option.

The Brontës are still inextricably linked to the village, and, almost 200 years on, remain its best known export. Their memory lives on in every nook and cranny – in cafes, bookshops, B&Bs and, of course, in the superb Parsonage Museum.

Haworth was home for the greater part of their lives and provided the setting – along with the surrounding moorland – for what many consider to be some of the world's finest romantic novels.

The family moved to the village in 1820 when their father was appointed curate at St Michael and All Angels Church. Charlotte, Emily and Anne and brother Branwell lived in the parsonage next to the church, taught at the village school and, in Branwell's case, drank in the local pubs.

At the parsonage, the Brontë sisters wrote novels which retain their ability to shock and inspire. Their most famous works – Charlotte's *Jane Eyre*, Anne's *The Tenant of Wildfell Hall* and Emily's *Wuthering Heights* – are in the literary DNA of generations of schoolchildren.

Our walk follows in the footsteps of the sisters who demonstrated in their writing both a remarkable sympathy for nature in the raw and an ability to withstand a fair amount of hardship. It takes in the parsonage, the so-called Brontë waterfalls, and, across Haworth Moor, Top Withens, inspiration for the Earnshaw family home in Wuthering Heights.

DISTANCE: 14KM/8.7MILES **TOTAL ASCENT**: 258M/850FT **START**: HAWORTH RAILWAY STATION (GR: SE 034 372)
TIME: 3 HOURS **MAP**: OS EXPLORER OL21: SOUTH PENNINES 1:25:000 **REFRESHMENTS**: PUBS IN STANBURY AND
TEAROOMS IN HAWORTH **NAVIGATION**: CLEAR TRACKS AND PATHS **SUGGESTED READING**: *WUTHERING
HEIGHTS*, EMILY BRONTË; *JANE EYRE*, CHARLOTTE BRONTË, *TENANT OF WILDFELL HALL*, ANNE BRONTË
(ALL PUBLISHED BY PENGUIN CLASSICS)

Directions – Haworth & the Moors

S→ From the station car park turn **right** and follow the road over the bridge as it ascends
steeply towards Haworth Main Street. On reaching the cobbled Main Street **walk up**
through the village until you reach St Michael and All Angels Church.

2 Go up the steps past the church and Brontë Parsonage, following the public footpath
signposted *To West Lane* and continuing along a stepping stone footpath through
private fields.

3 Turn **left** through the kissing gate and take the first **left** up Cemetery Road (keeping to
the footpath on the right hand side). **Ignore** the *Urban Common* signs and continue
along the path until you come to the main road.

4 Cross the road and take the private footpath marked *Footpath to Brontë Waterfalls* for
one and a half miles. The path will gradually descend and join stone steps to meet the
waterfalls.

5 Turn **right** over the bridge and take the path to your **left**, gradually climbing to a kissing
gate. Follow the path signposted *Top Withens* for almost one mile, passing through
fields and moorland before meeting another signpost denoting the 200-yard climb to
Top Withens.

6 **Retrace** your steps to the last signpost and take the path towards Stanbury and Haworth
where the path forms part of the Pennine Way. Shortly after passing a farmhouse turn
left down the path signposted *Haworth*.

7 On reaching the main road, turn **right** and walk along Back Lane through Stanbury.
The pavement is narrow and you will have to cross the road to walk safely through
the village.

8 As you leave Stanbury **ignore** the signpost for *Haworth* straight ahead and turn **right**
at the signpost for *Oxenhope*, crossing the reservoir bridge.

HAWORTH

Modern-day Haworth is unrecognisable from the place where the Brontë sisters grew up. It had the highest mortality rate outside London with the average age of death at the time just 25. By those standards, Anne, who died at the age of 29, Emily at 30, and Charlotte at 38, all lived beyond the usual span, perhaps a result of the family having their own water supply when most villagers drank water which had passed through the graveyard. There were two other Brontë sisters – Maria (said to be the cleverest of them all) and Elizabeth – both of whom died in childhood.

9 Cross the road carefully at the end of the bridge and take the path immediately to the **left** ascending to Cemetery Road. At the bottom of Cemetery Road turn **right**, go through the stile gate immediately on your **right** and follow the path back to the Brontë Parsonage.

10 **Retrace** your steps down Haworth Main Street and follow the main road as it winds its way down to the station car park.

TOP WITHENS

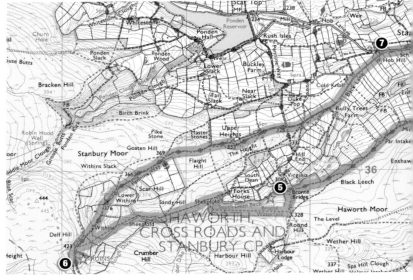

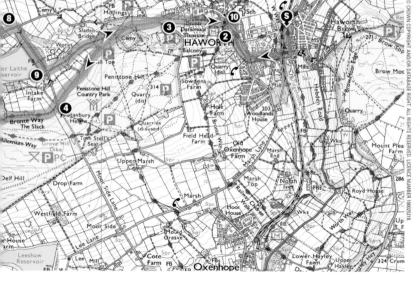

© CROWN COPYRIGHT AND/OR DATABASE RIGHT. ALL RIGHTS RESERVED. LICENCE NUMBER 100025218.

15 HAWORTH & THE MOORS

CHURN MILK JOAN

16 Mytholmroyd & the Calder Valley

(Ted Hughes)   **9.5km/6miles**

Exploring the moorland legend of Churn Milk Joan.

Mytholmroyd • Brearley • Midgley • Calderdale Way • Churn Milk Joan • Red Acre Wood • Mytholmroyd

START
Park in the car park at Mytholmroyd Community Centre, Elphaborough Hall, Streamside Fold. GR: SE 011 260.

THE WALK
Poet Ted Hughes never looked far beyond his native West Riding for inspiration for some of the finest verse ever written about the natural world.

Though he left Yorkshire to study at Cambridge and thereafter spent most of his adult life away, Hughes returned time and again in his poetry to the Calder Valley he knew as a child.

Our walk visits one of the places every youngster growing up in Mytholmroyd in the '30s would have known – if only for its unusual name.

Churn Milk Joan, a single standing stone on Midgley Moor, is reckoned to date back to 1600 and has accumulated a wealth of folklore ever since.

In his poem of the same name Hughes explores the legend of the stone (said to have been used as a collection point for milk produced at local farms) and the unfortunate Joan who came to a grisly end there one winter's night.

Today walkers maintain the tradition of Churn Milk Joan by replacing a coin left in the hollow of the stone – at one time the 'milk money' – with one of their own.

Tragically, Hughes is remembered today as much for his turbulent personal life as for the quality of the verse that saw him serve as Poet Laureate from 1984 until his death in 1998.

While at Cambridge he met and married Sylvia Plath, a young American student on a scholarship. After a brief spell in Plath's native Massachusetts, the couple returned to England but the marriage was unhappy and Plath committed suicide in 1962.

After her death Hughes did not write for many years and instead devoted his energy to promoting his late wife's work.

The walk starts in Mytholmroyd and passes through Brearley and Midgley before passing by Churn Milk Joan on the Calderdale Way and returning to Mytholmroyd through Red Acre Wood.

DISTANCE: 9.5KM/6MILES   **TOTAL ASCENT**: 290M/960FT   **START**: MYTHOLMROYD COMMUNITY CENTRE CAR
PARK (GR: SE 011 260)   **TIME**: 3 HOURS   **MAP**: OS EXPLORER OL21: SOUTH PENNINES 1:25:000
REFRESHMENTS: PUBS AND TEAROOMS IN MYTHOLMROYD   **NAVIGATION**: CLEAR PATHS, STRENUOUS IN PARTS
SUGGESTED READING: *REMAINS OF ELMET*, TED HUGHES (PUBLISHED BY FABER)

Directions – Mytholmroyd & the Calder Valley

S➤ From the community centre car park, turn **right** over a bridge, **right again** on to High Street and then first **right** signposted to Mytholmroyd train station (along New Road). At the train station go under the bridge and turn **left** up to the Manchester bound platform. Follow the cycle path **ahead** through woodland and continue along the path as it curves to the left then crosses a bridge over the railway line. Shortly afterwards you will pass the old Brearley Chapel on your right.

2 Turn **left** at Mill Hill and cross two bridges to reach the main road. Cross the road carefully and head **straight up** Brearley Lanes Top following the waymark signs for Churn Milk Joan. After a coppice of silver birches, look out for a small gap in the stone wall on the **right**, then follow the steps to make your ascent of more stone steps. There is a bench for a rest at the top!

3 Turn **right** to Midgley village and **right again** at Midgley junction. Take an **immediate left** up Chapel Lane past the old Methodist Church and graveyard. At the top of the lane, just past the stables, follow the path to the **left** and, as the path forks, take the steep narrow path up by a stone wall (signposted by waymarkers) and continue across the moorland.

4 Pass through a kissing gate signposted *Churn Milk* Joan circular walk and follow the footpath, alongside a fence and then **diagonally** across the moorland tracking waymarkers until you reach Churn Milk Joan.

5 Follow the path **left** and cross a step stile to your **left**. Follow the waymarkers across farmland over a number of ladder and step stiles. After crossing the final stile follow the path around a farmhouse, through a gate and down a road. Turn **right** to walk carefully along the main road.

6 After 750 metres, at High Road Cottage, turn **left** down a footpath. Then, after a cottage, turn **right** down stone steps marked by a Churn Milk Joan sign. As the path descends take an immediate **left** just before a stone cottage, crossing a stile. Continue to descend through a further stile and cross two streams.

ROCHDALE CANAL

The Rochdale Canal, which runs through Mytholmroyd, provided a source of poetic inspiration throughout Hughes's life. Childhood friends recall how they would fish the canal for tiddlers with a net, keeping their catch overnight in jam jars from the local Co-op. Hughes revisited the canal in two of his poems – *The Canal's Drowning Black*, in which he describes the wonder of catching a five-inch loach in the murky water, and *The Long Tunnel Ceiling*, in which he marvels at the sight of a leaping trout under the canal bridge.

7 Ascend and cross a stile, following the path through woodland. Pass through a metal kissing gate and take the path descending to the right down stone steps. Take the path to the **left** and continue **straight ahead**.

8 Pass through a metal gate and turn **right** over a canal bridge. At the main road turn **left** walking past the fire station. Cross the road at the pedestrian crossing and a second road to return to the community centre car park.

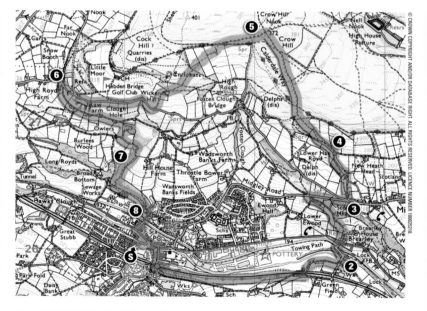

© CROWN COPYRIGHT AND/OR DATABASE RIGHT. ALL RIGHTS RESERVED. LICENCE NUMBER 100025218.

16 MYTHOLMROYD & THE CALDER VALLEY

APPROACH TO MAM TOR

17 Mam Tor & the Caverns
(Arthur Conan Doyle)

8km/5miles

A tour of Castleton's famous show caverns and the 'shivering mountain' Mam Tor.

Castleton • Speedwell Cavern • Treak Cliff Cavern • Blue John Cavern • Mam Tor • Castleton

START
Park at the Castleton Visitor Centre car park on Buxton Road. GR: SK 149 289.

THE WALK
Famous as the creator of Sherlock Holmes, Sir Arthur Conan Doyle started his career as a doctor in Edinburgh before finding popular success as an author.

The Terror of Blue John Gap was written by Conan Doyle after a convalescent stay in Castleton, Derbyshire. The short story was originally published in The Strand Magazine in 1910 and later as part of a collection of horror stories.

The tale is about a prehistoric beast that terrorises a village from its supposed lair in local caves. The main character, James Hardcastle, is – like Conan Doyle himself – a doctor hoping to recover from illness by taking in the fresh air of the Derbyshire hills.

The locals warn Dr Hardcastle to stay away from the caverns, blaming the sinister creature that lurks there for strange noises, blood trails and the disappearance of local animals.

Unperturbed, Dr Hardcastle investigates and, after a local farmer goes missing, decides to solve the mystery once and for all.

Dr Hardcastle dies shortly after his encounter with the 'terror' and the circumstances of his death remain unclear until a diary is found that recounts the events of his fateful stay.

Conan Doyle memorably described Castleton as 'hollow country' because of the number of caverns and show caves – 'could you strike it with some gigantic hammer, it would boom like a drum or possibly cave in altogether.'

Our walk starts in Castleton and takes in all four of the village's show caves. These include the Blue John Cavern of Conan Doyle's story where the Blue John semi-precious mineral is mined.

The walk continues on a steep climb up the 233 stone steps to the summit of Mam Tor, known locally as the 'shivering mountain' before returning to Castleton Village.

DISTANCE: 8KM/5 MILES   **TOTAL ASCENT**: 380M/1,246FT   **START**: CASTLETON VISITOR CENTRE CAR PARK
(GR: SK 149 829)   **TIME**: 2½ HOURS   **MAP**: OS EXPLORER OL1: THE PEAK DISTRICT – DARK PEAK AREA, 1:25,000
REFRESHMENTS: PUBS AND TEAROOMS IN CASTLETON   **NAVIGATION**: CLEAR PATHS BUT STEEP AND STRENUOUS
IN PARTS   **SUGGESTED READING**: *THE TERROR OF BLUE JOHN GAP*, SIR ARTHUR CONAN DOYLE: AVAILABLE AS
A FREE DOWNLOAD FROM: *HTTP://ETC.USF.EDU/LIT2GO*

Directions – Mam Tor & the Caverns

S→ From the car park, head to the main street, crossing the road at the Castle Hotel to walk up Castle Street. Turn **right** and follow the path signposted *Peak Cavern*.

2 **Follow** the path over a small stone bridge, and continue until you reach the houses. Just before the entrance to Peak Cavern, take an **immediate right** passing a cluster of cottages. At the junction, turn **left** past Dale House and follow the footpath signposted *Speedwell Cavern*.

3 Pass through a wooden gate along a stony path to a kissing gate. Cross the road adjacent to Speedwell Cavern and go through the gate immediately opposite. Follow the path across the field and through a small wooden gate marking a National Trust public footpath.

4 Follow the footpath towards Treak Cliff Cavern, climbing the stairs next to the cavern building, then take the path to the **immediate right**. Follow the path until you reach wooden gates. **Ignore** the path to your right and continue **straight** on until you reach Blue John Cavern.

5 Turn **left** past the cavern building, passing through a stile and follow the path as it climbs to a gate in the far right of the field. Continue **straight on** until you reach two gates on the perimeter wall. Pass through the gate on the **left**, crossing the road, and then pass through a further gate to reach a footpath signposted *Windy Knoll*.

6 Pass through a gate, cross a road and walk to the base of Mam Tor. Pass through two kissing gates and the National Trust Mam Tor sign before taking the 233 stone steps to the summit of the 'Shivering Mountain.'

7 From the summit, **follow** the stone footpath, passing through two gates until you reach a small monument to rambler Tom Hyett. Turn **right** here and take the path immediately to the **left** that crosses three stiles and a wooden gate as it descends. You will see an information board 'The View from the Liggate.'

BLUE JOHN

Castleton is the main centre for Derbyshire Blue John, a mineral used to make jugs, bowls, brooches and other decorative objects since the 18th century. The semi-precious stone was first discovered by miners looking for lead and at the height of its popularity there were 16 mines working the area. Ornaments and jewellery produced from Blue John would grace Windsor Castle, the White House and the Vatican, and some of the finest dining tables in the land. Today it is still extracted in small quantities from Treak Cliff and Blue John caverns at Castleton.

8 Continue along the road until Castleton comes into view and the road curves to the right.

9 Past a number of houses you will come to Millbridge. Here take the footpath adjacent to a house on the **right** (Brookhouse) and walk along the brook until you reach the car park at Castleton.

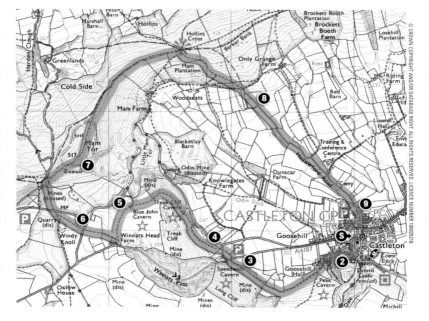

© CROWN COPYRIGHT AND/OR DATABASE RIGHT ALL RIGHTS RESERVED. LICENCE NUMBER 100023218.

17 MAM TOR & THE CAVERNS

18 Around Chatsworth
(Jane Austen)

8km/5miles

The view of Chatsworth House that provided the inspiration for Mr Darcy's country home in *Pride and Prejudice*.

Calton Lees • Chatsworth House • Edensor • Calton Lees

START
Park in Calton Lees car park (just before garden centre) on the west side of B6012. GR: SK 258 685.

THE WALK
Jane Austen declared that there was no finer county in England than Derbyshire. No surprise then that she chose Chatsworth House as the inspiration for her most famous – and unlikely – love match.

Austen first visited Chatsworth while staying in nearby Bakewell in 1811. At the time she was working on the novel which later became known as *Pride and Prejudice*.

Her impressions are not recorded. But in a famous passage from the novel she describes how Elizabeth Bennet came upon Pemberley, home of the wealthy and hitherto disagreeable Mr Darcy:

'They gradually ascended for half a mile, and then found themselves at the top of a considerable eminence, where the wood ceased, and the eye was instantly caught by Pemberley House situated on the opposite side of the valley, into which the road with some abruptness wound.'

If that description sounds familiar to lovers of the real-life Chatsworth so perhaps is Elizabeth's reaction.

'She had never seen a place for which nature had done more, or where natural beauty had been so little counteracted by an awkward taste.'

The magnificent pile works its magic on our heroine and the visit to Darcy's country home with her aunt and uncle proves to be the turning point in the book's central relationship. From that point on and pretty much against all expectations, Elizabeth is destined to become Mrs Darcy, mistress of Pemberley.

Chatsworth House (which is mentioned by name in the book) is today the home of the Duke and Duchess of Devonshire and has been in the Cavendish family since Bess of Harwick settled there in 1549.

Setting off from Calton Lees, our walk takes in a stroll through the estate along the River Derwent and up through Edensor Village, before ascending to admire the view described by Austen in *Pride and Prejudice*.

DISTANCE: 8KM/5MILES   **TOTAL ASCENT**: 119M/390FT   **START**: CALTON LEES CAR PARK (GR: SK 258 685)

TIME: 2 HOURS   **MAP**: OS EXPLORER OL24: THE PEAK DISTRICT – WHITE PEAK AREA, 1:25,000

REFRESHMENTS: TEAROOMS AT CHATSWORTH HOUSE, EDENSOR AND CALTON LEES   **NAVIGATION**: CLEAR PATHS AND TRACKS   **SUGGESTED READING**: *PRIDE AND PREJUDICE*, JANE AUSTEN (PUBLISHED BY WORDSWORTH EDITIONS)

Directions – Around Chatsworth

S➤ From Calton Lees car park **return to** and cross the main road at the cattle grid, following the path alongside the River Derwent past Chatsworth House until you reach a bridge.

2 Cross the road at the bridge and follow the footpath **bearing left** towards Edensor (**ignoring** the entrance to the grounds of Chatsworth House). At Edensor Village cross the road and pass through blue gates, following the path through the centre of the village past the Church of St Peter and a number of picturesque cottages.

3 As you pass the cottages look out for a blue hand-painted sign on the **left** marked *Footpath to Calton Lees and Rowley*. Here follow the steep stone steps up to a footpath and a small iron gate.

If you continue to see a field to your left and woodland ahead you have gone too far. Retrace your footsteps and look out for the signpost and stone steps amongst the cottages.

4 Go through the iron gate and follow the public footpath as it crosses diagonally across the field (clearly signposted by markers). Continue uphill until you reach a stone wall around woodland. There are a number of wooden benches here allowing you to look back and enjoy the view of Chatsworth House as described by Austen.

5 Pass through the gate in the wall and follow the footpath through two wooden gates. The path crosses through the middle of the field before sloping to the right, descending to meet a third wooden gate.

6 Follow the footpath through the gate, passing Calton House and Barn as it winds down past the River Derwent.

7 After passing Grafton and Jasmine Cottages continue along the footpath which will take you back to your starting point at Calton Lees car park.

CHATSWORTH

Chatsworth has a library of some 30,000 books, among them more than 100 'dummy' books used to disguise doorways. The so-called 'invisible library' complete with fake bookshelves was a fashion in the mid to late 19th century – Charles Dickens commissioned one at his home in Tavistock Place – and generated a good deal of schoolboy humour when it came to choosing titles for the books. 'Intuition by Ivor Hunch' is one example of the genre, and 'Reduced to the Rank by D Motion', another.

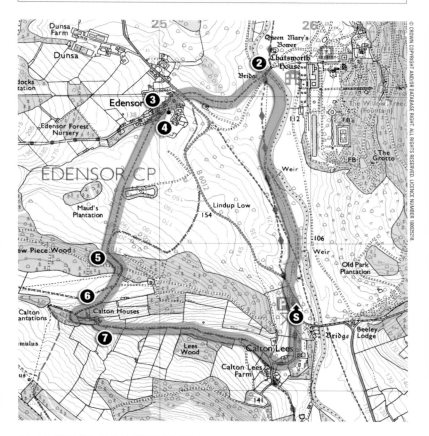

© CROWN COPYRIGHT AND/OR DATABASE RIGHT ALL RIGHTS RESERVED. LICENCE NUMBER 100025218.

18 AROUND CHATSWORTH

GASKELL TOWER

19 Knutsford & Tatton Park
(Elizabeth Gaskell)

11km/7miles

Around and about the real-life Cranford.

Knutsford • The Heath • Tatton Mere • Tatton Park • Knutsford

START
Park in Tatton Street car park, next to the Laura Ashley store on Tatton Street. GR: SJ 750 789.

THE WALK
She was born Elizabeth Cleghorn Stevenson, daughter of a Unitarian minister, in Chelsea in 1810. But she is best known as simply Mrs Gaskell.

The brilliant chronicler of Northern life is today most associated with the Cheshire town of Knutsford where she was brought at the age of just 13 months following the sudden death of her mother.

Here, in this affluent market town, Elizabeth grew up in the care of her aunt and here too at St John's Parish Church she married William Gaskell, a local man, writer, poet and later minister at Cross Street Unitarian Chapel in Manchester.

Mrs Gaskell always acknowledged the profound impact Knutsford made on her, describing it as her 'dear adopted, native town.' But it was through her writing that she brought its streets and shops to life, immortalising the town in two of her most famous works.

Cranford was published first in serial format in *Household Words*, a magazine edited by Charles Dickens, and later as a novella. It portrays the life of narrator Mary Smith and her close circle of friends in a Victorian country village.

In *Wives and Daughters, a tale of provincial life*, Knutsford becomes Hollingford and nearby Tatton Park, Cumnor Towers, home of the aristocratic Cumnor family. Mrs Gaskell fell ill and died before finishing the novel and Frederick Greenwood, editor of the *Pall Mall Gazette*, completed it.

As a novelist and biographer, Mrs Gaskell was popular and well respected among her peers and was close friends with Charles Kingsley, John Ruskin and the Brontë family. Her biography of Charlotte Brontë, published in 1857, remains to this day the definitive work on the author of *Jane Eyre*.

Our walk takes in the Knutsford of Mrs Gaskell's upbringing and passes her childhood home, the church in which she married, and sights familiar to readers of *Cranford* and *Wives and Daughters*, including Miss Matty's House and Cumnor Towers.

DISTANCE: 11KM/7MILES **TOTAL ASCENT**: 50M/164FT **START**: TATTON STREET CAR PARK WA16 6AG
(GR: SJ 750 789) **TIME**: 2½ HOURS **MAP**: OS EXPLORER OL268: WILMSLOW, MACCLESFIELD AND CONGLETON,
1:25:000 **REFRESHMENTS**: PUBS AND TEAROOMS IN KNUTSFORD AND TATTON PARK **NAVIGATION**: CLEAR
PATHS, FLAT AND SUITABLE FOR ALL ABILITIES **SUGGESTED READING**: *CRANFORD AND SELECTED SHORT STORIES,
WIVES AND DAUGHTERS*, ELIZABETH GASKELL (PUBLISHED BY WORDSWORTH CLASSICS)

Directions – Knutsford & Tatton Park

S➜ Turn **right** out of the car park and follow the road as it curves right to a roundabout.
Cross the road at the zebra crossing by the car showroom and head **left** up Northwich
Road, with Knutsford Heath to your right and a small common on the left.

2 Cross the road where the common ends, and turn **left** down Stanley Avenue, past
Cranford Avenue and turn **left** again up Gaskell Avenue. Keep to the right hand side of
the road, where you will pass Heathwaite House – Elizabeth Gaskell's home from 1811.

3 At the top of Gaskell Avenue, cross at the zebra crossing, pass the White Bear pub and
take the first road on the **right**, Princes Street. As you continue **straight on**, you will
pass a blue heritage plaque for Miss Matty's House (WH Smith). Turn **left** after passing
the Old Town Hall building, down Church Hill, passing St John's Baptist Church where
the Gaskells married, and continue down a short cobbled slope before turning **left**
onto King Street.

At the Belle Epoque Brasserie stop to admire the Gaskell Memorial Tower designed by
Richard Harding Watt, which commemorates Gaskell's works.

4 At the top of King Street, turn **right** and follow the path into Tatton Park, passing
through the stone archway. Follow the main path until it branches to the right and
continue to walk alongside Tatton Mere, passing a stone dam and going through a
kissing gate. **Ignore** the paths to left and right and carry **straight on**, walking through
the Old Hall car park. Keep to the public footpath as you pass the Old Hall to your right
and the deer park on your left.

5 Continue along the footpath until you reach a fork in the path. Here take a **left** to
cross a field with a coppice of trees to your left. As the path forks again, **continue left**,
walking around a small pond and keeping a fence to your left.

GASKELL MEMORIAL TOWER

The most visible reference to Mrs Gaskell in Knutsford is the Memorial Tower, a Grade II listed building in King Street built in 1907. It started life as the King's Coffee House but also housed a library and put on concerts and musical evenings to win working men away from the pub. The original menu stated that 'a warm bath may be had at any hour for sixpence.' Architect Richard Harding Watt said that Gaskell's works had given him great pleasure and it was right that she should be remembered in the town where she grew up.

6 Follow the footpath until you reach the main road into the park and turn **left** to walk up to the Mansion House (Cumnor Towers in Wives and Daughters). Go through an iron gate and arch in the hedge to visit the stable yard where there is a restaurant and farm shop.

7 **Return** to the front of the Mansion House and follow the main path back out of Tatton Park. Through the stone archway take the path to the **left**. Cross the road opposite a Laura Ashley shop to return to the car park.

HEATHWAITE HOUSE, GASKELL AVENUE (PRIVATE PROPERTY)

This property built in the
reign of George I is reputed
to have been the fictional home of
Miss Matty
the principal character in
Mrs Gaskell's 'Cranford'
and was also the home of
Miss Elizabeth Harker upon whom
Mrs Gaskell based her
'Cranford' character
Betty Barker.

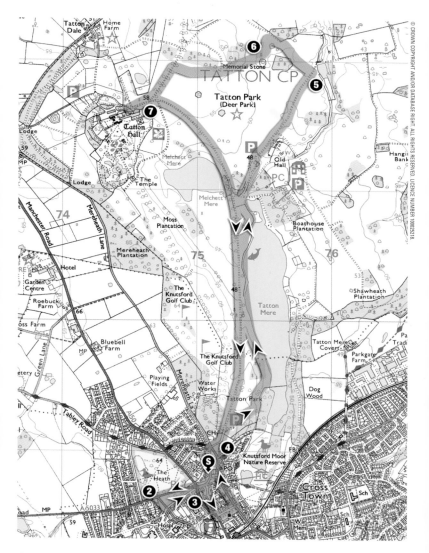

19 KNUTSFORD & TATTON PARK

© CROWN COPYRIGHT AND/OR DATABASE RIGHT. ALL RIGHTS RESERVED. LICENCE NUMBER 100025218.

20 Daresbury
(Lewis Carroll)

8km/5miles

A stroll round the Cheshire village and surroundings where Alice in Wonderland's creator grew up.

Daresbury • Daresbury Firs • Bridgewater Canal • Moore • Walton • Daresbury

START

Park at the Lewis Carroll Centre at All Saints Church on the B5356 Daresbury Lane in Daresbury. GR: SJ 580 828.

THE WALK

Lewis Carroll's best known books inhabit a world far removed from that known by the studious young Charles Lutwidge Dodgson growing up in rural Cheshire in the 1830s.

But today's visitors to Daresbury are left in little doubt of the links with the vicar's son who reinvented the art of storytelling for generations of children.

The Lewis Carroll Centre, part of All Saints Church, celebrates the fertile imagination of the poet and author who created *Alice's Adventures in Wonderland*, and pioneered the genre of literary nonsense in works like *Jabberwocky* and *The Hunting of the Snark*.

Dodgson was a talented mathematician, receiving a double first in mathematics from Christ Church, Oxford, and teaching there under his real name.

But he pursued a range of other interests, including photography and writing, and befriended John Ruskin and a number of artists from the Pre-Raphaelite Movement.

It was through a friendship with the Dean of Christ Church's niece that he got to know Alice Liddell, inspiration for one of the most famous characters in children's literature.

The story goes that it was on a boat trip with the real Alice and her two sisters that that he invented a fantastic story about a girl and a white rabbit to keep the young people amused.

Our walk starts from the Lewis Carroll Centre at All Saints Church, Daresbury and follows the Lewis Carroll trail through Daresbury, Firs Wood, and along the Bridgewater Canal to Moore, before returning to Daresbury Village.

Watch out for the carving of a Cheshire cat on the barn as you pass Rose Cottage. Local legend has it that the phrase 'to grin like a Cheshire cat' has its origins in the large number of dairy farms around here, a happy accident for the local cat population in search of milk and cream.

It was clearly a story that made its mark on the young Charles Dodgson.

DISTANCE: 8KM/5MILES **TOTAL ASCENT**: 20M/65FT **START**: LEWIS CARROLL CENTRE, ALL SAINTS CHURCH, DARESBURY (GR: SJ 580 828) **TIME**: 2 HOURS **MAP**: OS EXPLORER 267: NORTHWICH AND DELAMERE FOREST, 1:25,000 **REFRESHMENTS**: RING O'BELLS PUB, DARESBURY VILLAGE **NAVIGATION**: CLEAR PATHS BUT CROSSES SOME BUSY ROADS **SUGGESTED READING**: *ALICE'S ADVENTURES IN WONDERLAND*, LEWIS CARROLL (PUBLISHED BY COLLECTOR'S LIBRARY)

Directions – Daresbury

S➤ From the Lewis Carroll Centre on Daresbury Lane, turn **left** towards Hatton and then **right** passing through a kissing gate along a path signposted *Newton Lane ³/₄ mile, Lewis Carroll Walk*. Follow the path as it runs diagonally through a field towards a kissing gate in the far right corner.

2 Pass through the kissing gate and follow the path to the right hand side of the field. Halfway along, cross a stile and follow the sign marked *Daresbury village ¹/₄ mile*. Continue **straight on**, passing through a kissing gate and turning **right** to walk down Old Chester Road past Daresbury Primary School on the left. Turn **left** to follow the footpath just in front of Rose Cottage (signposted *Daresbury Firs*).

3 Continue along the path, following the sign marked *Mersey Valley Timberland Trail*. Pass through a kissing gate leading to a dual carriageway. Cross the road **carefully** to a kissing gate and walk through a field to pass through a second kissing gate.

4 Enter Daresbury Firs, taking the path to the **left** by an information board. Follow the signs for the *Mersey Valley Timberland Trail and Firs Woodland Walk*. The path descends through the wood, heading towards a field at the bottom of the valley. Follow the path to the left of the field and leave the wood through a kissing gate.

5 Turn **right** and cross a stone bridge over the Bridgewater Canal, taking an **immediate right** to join the towpath, and then **left** to walk with the canal on the right hand side – signposted *Moore*. Continue along the towpath, past Daresbury Science Park and under two canal bridges – Keckwick Bridge and Moorfield Bridge. Just before Moore Bridge leave the towpath, following the path to the **right**. Turn **right** and **right again** to cross Moore Bridge onto Hobb Lane. Walk through the village of Walton until you reach the main road.

6 **Cross carefully** and **straight ahead**, opposite the White House at the top of Hobb Lane, pass through a kissing gate and follow the public footpath towards woodland. Follow the path to the right along the perimeter of the woods, passing a pond on the right, to a kissing gate.

A TALE OF TWO NAMES

Charles Lutwidge Dodgson was a talented mathematician who lectured at Christ Church, Oxford, and wrote a number of books on mathematics and logic. But he went to great lengths to ensure that people did not associate the serious mathematician with Lewis Carroll, the creator of Alice and her fantastic companions. Dodgson never publicly acknowledged the connection to Lewis Carroll (a name derived from a Latin translation of Lutwidge Charles) and even sent correspondents an official disclaimer denying any association between his two personae.

7 Through the gate turn **left** and follow the path around the outside of the field towards a kissing gate in the far corner. Through the kissing gate follow the lane **straight ahead** and where the lane forks continue to the **left**, passing Daresbury Equestrian Centre.

8 At the end of the lane follow the path through a snicket to the **left** to meet Daresbury Road. Turn **right** passing Daresbury Hall before returning to the Lewis Carroll Centre.

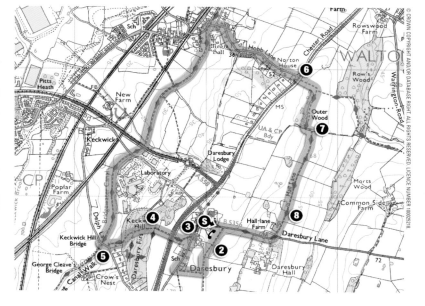

© CROWN COPYRIGHT AND/OR DATABASE RIGHT. ALL RIGHTS RESERVED. LICENCE NUMBER 100025218.

20 DARESBURY

APPENDIX

The following is a list of Tourist Information Centres, cafes, pubs, websites and other contacts that might come in handy.

TOURIST INFORMATION CENTRES

LAKE DISTRICT
www.lakedistrict.gov.uk (official website of the Lake District National Park)
Coniston t: 01539 441 533
Keswick t: 01768 772 645
Windermere t: 01539 446 499

NORTHUMBERLAND
www.northumberlandnationalpark.org.uk (official website of the Northumberland National Park)
Wooler t: 01668 282 123
Hexham t: 01434 652 220
South Shields t: 01914 546 612

NORTH YORK MOORS
www.northyorkmoors.org.uk (official website of the North York Moors National Park)
Whitby t: 01723 383 636
Thirsk t: 01845 522 755

PEAK DISTRICT
www.peakdistrict.gov.uk (official website of the Peak District National Park)
Castleton t: 01629 816 572

YORKSHIRE DALES
www.yorkshiredales.org.uk (official website of the Yorkshire Dales National Park)
Malham t: 01729 833 200
Grassington t: 01756 751 690

WEST YORKSHIRE
Haworth t: 01535 642 329
Hebden Bridge t: 01422 843 831

LANCASHIRE
Clitheroe t: 01200 425 566

FOOD & DRINK

CAFES (See individual routes for recommendations)

10 The Coffee House, Main Street, Haworth .... t: 01535 644 694
Courtyard Coffee House, rear 92 King Street, Knutsford .... t: 01565 653 974
The Old Barn, Malham .... t: 01729 830 486
Cote How Tearoom, Rydal .... t: 01539 432 765
The Old Saw Mill Tearoom, Mirehouse .... t: 01768 774 317
The White Monk Tearoom, Blanchland .... t: 01434 675 044
The Magpie Café, 14 Pier Road, Whitby .... t: 01947 602 058

PUBS (See individual routes for recommendations)

The Dusty Miller, Burnley Road, Mytholmroyd .... t: 01422 885 959
The Castle Inn, Castle Street, Castleton .... t 01433 620 578
The Cuckoo Brow Inn, Far Sawrey .... t: 01539 443 425
The Mill Inn, Mungrisdale .... t: 01768 779 632
The Wilson Arms, Torver .... t: 01539 441 237
The George Inn, Hubberholme .... t: 01756 760 223
The Bayley Arms, Hurst Green .... t: 01254 826 478

ACCOMMODATION

For specific information about a particular area contact the relevant Tourist Information Centre

WEATHER

www.metoffice.gov.uk

PUBLIC TRANSPORT

Many of the starting points for our walks are accessible by bus or train.
www.nationalrail.co.uk
http://traveline.info

OTHER CONTACTS

Cumbria Tourism .... www.golakes.co.uk
Northumberland Tourism .... www.visitnorthumberland.com
Yorkshire Tourism .... www.yorkshire.com
Peak District Tourism .... www.visitpeakdistrict.com
Cheshire Tourism .... www.visitchester.com
Lancashire Tourism .... www.visitlancashire.com

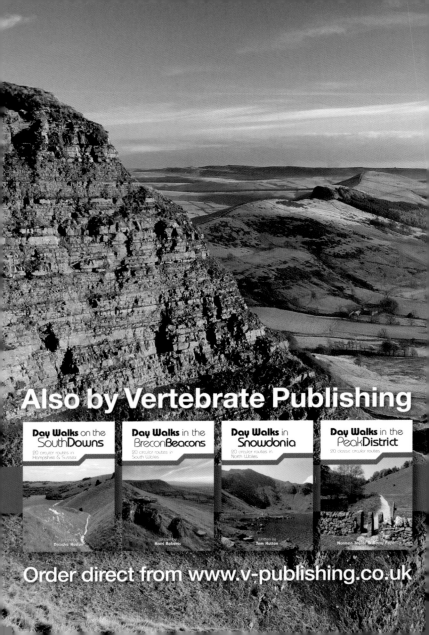

Also by Vertebrate Publishing

Day Walks on the SouthDowns
20 circular routes in Hampshire & Sussex

Day Walks in the BreconBeacons
20 circular routes in South Wales

Day Walks in Snowdonia
20 circular routes in North Wales

Day Walks in the PeakDistrict
20 classic circular routes

Written by Deirdre Huston

Written by Harri Roberts

Written by Tom Hutton

Norman Taylor & Barry Pope

Order direct from www.v-publishing.co.uk

Written by local authors, each book features:

» 20 great day-length circular walks
» Invaluable local area information
» Ordnance Survey maps
» Easy-to-use directions

Day Walks in the
PeakDistrict
20 New Circular Routes

Written by
Norman Taylor & Barry Pope

Day Walks in the
YorkshireDales
20 circular routes in the
Central Pennines

Written by
Bernard Newman

Day Walks in the
North York Moors
20 circular routes in
North Yorkshire

Written by
Tony Harker

Day Walks in the
LakeDistrict
20 circular routes on
the Lakeland Fells

Written by
Stephen Goodwin

PHOTO BY: GILL SALIM

ABOUT THE AUTHORS

Ian Hamilton is a former journalist who worked on a number of local newspapers in Yorkshire and Lancashire. He peaked as a long distance walker at the age of 13 when he completed the Lyke Wake Walk in daylight hours, a feat he seems unlikely to repeat. Today he prefers shorter, less demanding expeditions, and is among the growing band of people who would like to keep the delights of the Trough of Bowland secret from the rest of the world. Ian is married to Ann and has three grown-up children.

Diane Roberts started serious walking while at university in Scotland and today combines her love of the outdoors with a passion for photography. She has an affinity for the landscapes that inspired our greatest writers – and the teashops that often spring up in their wake. Diane works for the civil service in Manchester and was previously part of the team that helped to bring the BBC to her native Salford. She lives with her partner Dave and their Italian greyhound Reggie.